Supporting SOCIAL-EMOTIONAL LEARNING
With Remote Instruction

Gerry Dunne, Ph.D. & Susanna Palomares, M.Ed.

INNERCHOICE Publishing

Cover design: Dave Cowan

Copyright 2020, Innerchoice Publishing • All rights reserved

ISBN-10: 1-56499-101-6

ISBN-13: [

INNERCHOICE Publishing
15079 Oak Chase Court
Wellington, FL 33414

www.InnerchoicePublishing.com

Reproduction by any means or for any purpose whatsoever, is explicitly prohibited without written permission. Requests for permission should be directed to INNERCHOICE PUBLISHING.

Contents

Introduction... 1

Activities.. 13

How My Life Has Changed Because of the Pandemic................ 15

What I Like About Distance Learning 16

What I Don't Like About Distance Learning 17

What I Miss Most About Being in School 18

Someone (or Something) at Home That Helps Me Feel Okay 19

What's Stressing Me Out and How I Handle It 20

Words That Help Me Feel Safe and Secure 22

My Hopeful Visions for the Future............................. 23

My Favorite Place... 24

A Time When I Felt Happy...................................... 25

One of My Favorite Possessions................................ 26

My Favorite Game 27

My Favorite Movie or TV Show.................................. 28

A Time When Something Funny Happened 30

A Favorite Book (or Story)	32
Something I Like to Daydream About	33
What I Would Do If I Were Made King or Queen of the World for One Day	34
Something That I Think Is Beautiful	35
A Smile from Someone Special	36
Something I'm Looking Forward To	38
A Rule We Have In My Family	39
One of the Best Times I Ever Had With My Family	40
An Important Person In My Life	42
A Way I Show Respect For Others	43
I Have a Friend Who Is Different from Me	44
How I React When I'm Happy	45
How I Made Someone Feel Happy	46
A Time I Managed My Anger	48
It Was Difficult, But I Controlled Myself	50
How I Like to Spend My Free Time	51
An Adventure I Had	52
My Favorite Musical Group	53
A Hero or Heroine I Admire	54
If I Could Do Anything I Wanted	55
What People Need from Each Other In Order to Be Good Friends	56
A Person I Feel Safe With	57
A Place Where I Feel Safe	58
Someone Who Trusts Me	60
Someone I Don't Trust Very Much	61
How I Show Someone That They Can Trust Me	62

A Time When I Trusted Myself, or I Knew I Could Do It	64
I Taught Myself Something	65
The Way I Learn Best	66
Something I Learned That Was Enjoyable	68
Something I'm Learning About Now That is Hard	69
A Time When Someone Listened Well to Me	70
Once When Someone Wouldn't Listen to Me	71
A Time When I Listened Well to Someone	72
A Time When We Communicated Without Words	74
How I Let Others Know That I Am Interested in What They Say	76
A Name I'd Like to Have	77
If I Were an Animal	78
A Person I'd Like to Be Like	79
Someone Who Demonstrates a Lot of Courage	80
A Group I Like Belonging To	81
Who I Am Culturally	82
A Special Occasion or Holiday That Relates to My Culture	84
Something I Like That Is Part of Another Culture	85
I Helped Someone Who Wanted My Help	86
Someone Helped Me When I Wanted to Be Helped	87
I Got Some Help I Didn't Want	88
I Asked for Help When I Needed It	89
I Helped Someone Even Though I Didn't Feel Like It	90
A Way in Which I'm Responsible	91
Something I Worked Hard At	92
Something I Do Well That I Like to Do	93

Something I Did (or Made) That I'm Proud Of 94

Something That I Want to Do (or Make) Someday
That I Haven't Done Yet 95

Something Worth Saving Money For 96

Something That I Like to Do Now That Could
Relate to My Job When I'm An Adult 98

What I Value In a Friend 100

One of the Best Times I Ever Had With a Friend 101

Something I Never Do When I Want to Make Friends With Someone . . 102

One of the Nicest Things A Friend Ever Did for Me 103

Something Nice That I Did For a Friend 104

My Friend (or Friends) Tried to Make Me Do
Something I Didn't Want to Do 105

I Reached Out to Someone When I Knew They Needed a Friend 106

When I Was The One Who Needed a Friend 107

When My Friend Moved Away 108

Something That Annoys Me 109

A Time When I Was Disappointed 110

A Time I Disappointed Someone 111

How I Would Solve Somebody Else's Problem 112

A Problem I'm Still Trying to Solve 114

I Had a Problem I Solved In a Positive Way 116

I Made a Decision That Was Easy to Make 117

When I Did Not Get to Share In Making The Decision 118

When I Got to Share In Making The Decision 119

I Didn't Want to Have to Make a Decision 120

I Stuck By a Difficult Decision I Made 121

I Thought It Over and Then Decided 122

I Observed a Conflict 124

I Got Blamed for Something That I Didn't Do. 127

I Got Involved In a Conflict Because Something Unfair
Was Happening to Someone Else 128

I Got Into a Fight Because I Was Already Feeling Bad 129

I Felt Like Saying Something, but I Didn't 130

A Time When Somebody Put Me Down and I Handled It Well 131

I Was Angry At One Person, but I Took It Out On Someone Else 132

A Good Idea I Got From Someone In the Group
for Handling a Conflict 134

Something I've Done (or Could Do) to Improve Our World 135

Introduction

SUPPORTING SEL WITH DISTANCE LEARNING

Relationships are the heart of social emotional learning, but with many schools currently offering remote learning instruction establishing supportive, caring relationships is a big challenge. The Sharing Circle process has been used for decades in classrooms and counseling groups to create a sense of community and to lay the foundation of a safe, caring learning environment while also specifically teaching such SEL skills as self-awareness, self-management, social-awareness, and relationship skills. In Sharing Circles the students and their teacher (or counselor) get to know each other on a meaningful, supportive level while discussing relevant topics dealing with the wide range of social emotional skill development.

A key avenue to maintaining and enhancing our social and emotional lives is through the process of verbal interaction. Even with the social restrictions imposed on us by the COVID pandemic, with our complex emotional and relational lives, it would be devastating if we couldn't talk with others about such things as our experiences, feelings, hopes, fears, desires etc. When we do share our experiences and feelings at a level beyond superficiality, we come to realize that all of us not only experience all of the emotions and feelings, but that we each experience them in our own unique ways. By sharing meaningful experiences and feelings in a safe space we are enabled to see the basic commonalities among us, and the individual differences too. This understanding leads to self-awareness and self-respect. On this foundation we can then develop empathy and concern for others as well. The benefits of time devoted to Sharing Circles, whether online or in person, is a growing awareness of self and an understanding of the importance of effectively relating to others.

HOW SHARING CIRCLES TEACH SOCIAL AND EMOTIONAL LEARNING

As students follow the rules and relate to each other verbally during the Sharing Circle, they are practicing respectful listening and oral communication. As they listen carefully while other students and their teacher or counselor ponder and discuss the various topics, the students have repeated opportunities to mentally take the perspective of others. In doing so they grow to understand that others have joys and pains and fears just as they do. This lays the foundation for developing empathy and kindness. The ground rules also require them to demonstrate awareness and control over their own feelings, thoughts, and behaviors during the discussion. Through this repeated experience of positive give and take, they learn the importance of interacting responsibly and effectively while also practicing the valuable skill of self-management.

The topics provided in this book address many qualities inherent in people with well developed social and emotional skills— keeping agreements, developing responsible habits, solving problems, demonstrating respect for self and others, being loyal, being trustworthy and honest, following rules, demonstrating kindness and consideration, resolving conflicts, etc. By discussing this wide range of life skill topics, and considering their impact, the students develop awareness and insight regarding the value of these qualities in their own lives.

As students learn to relate effectively to others, issues related to acceptable and unacceptable behavior surface again and again. Students learn that all people have the power to influence one another. They become aware not only of how others affect them, but of the effects their behaviors have on others.

All students bring their own cultural and individual experiences to school. Whether virtual or in person, Sharing Circles provide an ideal way to give everyone repeated opportunities to express and share their individuality in a safe and accepting environment. When young people from differing cultural backgrounds, abilities and gender identities share truthful, respectful and meaningful discussions, it breaks down unconscious biases and fosters relationships and understanding. This is the true spirit of community building. In the Sharing Circle respect is always given and individual differences and cultural backgrounds are recognized and valued. Additionally, by getting to know their students in such a meaningful and personal way teachers and counselors can identify unique skills and experiences to build upon and areas of growth and needed support.

The Sharing Circle process has been designed so that healthy, responsible behaviors are modeled by the teacher or counselor in their role as the Sharing Circle leader. Also, the rules require that the students relate responsibly and effectively to one another. The process brings out and affirms the positive qualities inherent in everyone and allows students to practice effective modes of communication. Because Sharing Circles provide a place where participants are listened to and their feelings accepted, students learn how to provide the same conditions to peers and adults in interactions beyond the Sharing Circle sessions.

Sharing Circles teach cooperation and promote caring. As equitably as possible, the structure attempts to meet the needs of all participants. Everyone's feelings are accepted; everyone's contributions are judged valuable. The Sharing Circle is not another competitive arena, but is guided by a spirit of collaboration. When students practice fair, respectful interaction with one another, they benefit from the experience and are likely to employ these responsible behaviors in other life situations.

HOW TO CONDUCT SHARING CIRCLES

This book presents the successful Sharing Circle approach to social and emotional learning in an adapted format that works simply and effectively in a distance learning environment. If you are using a hybrid model of teaching and want to also implement the Sharing Circle in your classroom, the same rules and procedure apply. In the classroom, keeping distance guidelines in mind, you would want to have the students sitting in a circle so everyone can see everyone else. Not looking at the back of someone's head.

The focus of this section is a thorough guide for conducting Sharing Circles remotely. It covers major points to keep in mind and answers questions which will arise as you begin using the program. Please remember that these guidelines are presented to assist you, not to restrict you. Follow them, and trust your own teaching style at the same time.

First, we'll provide a brief overview of the process of leading a Sharing Circle and then we'll cover each step in more detail.

A Sharing Circle begins when a group of students and their teacher, or counselor, meet together in a group. Zoom is a popular and workable program to use for this approach. With a group of 12 or fewer everyone can be seen by everyone else just as they would in an in-person circle. The teacher briefly greets and welcomes the students, conveying a feeling of enthusiasm blended with seriousness.

During the first few sessions and while the students are still learning about the rules, the teacher takes a few moments to review the rules. These rules inform the students of the positive behaviors required of them and guarantees the emotional safety and security, and equality of each member.

When everyone has settled in and after the students understand and agree to follow the rules, the teacher announces the topic for the session. A brief elaboration of the topic follows in which the teacher provides examples and possibly mentions the topics relationship to prior topics or to other things the students are involved in. Then the teacher re-states the topic and allows a little silence during which the students may review and ponder their own related memories and mentally prepare their verbal response to the topic. (The topics and brief elaborations are provided in this book.)

Next, the teacher invites the students to voluntarily share their responses to the topic, one at a time. No one is forced to share (because it's okay to pass) but everyone is given an opportunity to share while all the other group members listen attentively. The participants tell the group about themselves, their personal experiences, thoughts, feelings, hopes and dreams as they relate to the topic. The most time in each session is devoted to this sharing phase because of its central importance.

During this time, the teacher assumes a dual role—that of leader and participant. The leader makes sure that everyone who wishes to speak is given the opportunity while simultaneously enforcing the rules as necessary. The leader also takes a turn to speak if they wish.

After everyone who wants to share has done so, the teacher introduces the next phase of the Sharing Circle by asking several discussion questions. This phase represents a transition to the intellectual mode and allows participants to reflect on and express learnings gained from the sharing phase and encourages participants to combine cognitive abilities and emotional experiencing. It's in this phase that participants are able to crystallize learnings and to understand the relevance of the discussion to their daily lives. (Discussion questions for each topic are provided in this book.)

When the students have finished discussing their responses to the questions and the session has reached a natural closure, the teacher ends the session by thanking the students for being part of the Sharing Circle and stating that it is over.

Here is a more detailed look at the process of leading a Sharing Circle.

Steps for Leading a Sharing Circle

1. Welcome group members
2. Review the Sharing Circle rules *
3. Introduce the topic
4. Sharing by circle members
5. Ask discussion questions
6. Close the circle

  *optional after the first few sessions

---

1. Welcome group members

The Sharing Circle provides a threat-free atmosphere where the students can explore their own feelings, thoughts and behaviors and consider those of the other members of the group. When you exhibit a positive, warm, and enthusiastic attitude, the students will know that this group is an important part of the day's learning experience, and most importantly that you care about them as individuals. By using the following communication techniques it will help to establish the rapport you are seeking and provide the foundation of a caring, supportive relationship.

- Use their names
- Show them that you are listening and hear what they are saying
- Let them know you think highly of them and their willingness to participate
- Make a conscientious effort to promote self-esteem and confidence. The Sharing Circle is a place where everyone has the "right" answer and should always feel successful in their participation whether by speaking or simply listening.

2. Review the Sharing Circle rules

At the beginning of the first few sessions, and if necessary at intervals thereafter, go over the ground rules. They are:

Sharing Circle Rules

- Everyone gets a turn to share, including the leader.
- You can skip your turn if you wish.
- Listen to the person who is sharing.
- There are no interruptions, put-downs, or gossip.
- Share the time equally so everyone gets a turn to speak.

From this point on demonstrate to the students that you expect them to remember and abide by these rules. Convey to the students that you think well of them and know they are fully capable of responsible behavior. Let them know that by coming to the group they are making a commitment to listen and show acceptance and respect for the other students and you. It can be helpful to write the rules in the chat box so the students can see, as well as hear, the rules while they are learning what they are. For in-person classroom sessions display the rules on the board or chart paper.

3. Introduce the topic

State the topic and, then in your own words, elaborate and provide examples as each Sharing Circle lesson suggests. The topic can be written in the chat box so that the students can review the topic as they need throughout the session. You may want to expand your elaboration beyond the brief suggestions provided with more examples. This elaboration of the topic is designed to get students focused and thinking about how they will respond to the topic. By providing more than just the mere statement of the topic, the elaboration gives students a few moments to expand their thinking and to make a personal connection to the topic at hand. Add clarifying statements of your own that will help the students understand the topic. Answer questions about the topic, and emphasize that there are no "right" or "wrong" responses. Finally, open the session to responses (theirs and yours). Sometimes taking your turn first helps the students understand the aim of the topic. The Sharing Circle elaborations, as written in this book, are provided to give you some general ideas for opening the Sharing Circle. It's important that you adjust, expand and modify the elaboration to suit the ages, abilities, levels, cultural/ethnic backgrounds and interests of your students.

4. Sharing by circle members

The most important point to remember is this: The purpose of these Sharing Circles is to give students an opportunity to express themselves and be accepted for the experiences, thoughts, and feelings they share. Keep the focus on the students. They are the stars!

5. Ask discussion questions

Responding to discussion questions is the cognitive portion of the process. During this phase, the teacher asks thought-provoking questions to stimulate free discussion and higher-level thinking. As John Dewey, the early 20th century educational leader and reformer said "We do not learn from experience, we learn from reflecting on experience". Each Sharing Circle lesson concludes with several culminating discussion questions designed to foster reflection and self-awareness. You may want to formulate your own questions that are based on students' responses, relevant learning's you would like to focus on, or that are more appropriate to the level of understanding in your students. Use your professional judgment to determine exactly what questions to ask.

6. Close the circle

The ideal time to end a session is when the discussion question phase reaches natural closure. Sincerely thank everyone for being part of the group. Don't thank specific students for speaking, as doing so might convey the impression that speaking is more appreciated than listening. As the directions with each Sharing Circle in this book suggests you could also thank the students for positive behaviors that were demonstrated during the session.

More about Sharing Circle Steps and Rules

The next few paragraphs offer further clarification concerning leadership of Sharing Circles.

Who gets to talk? Everyone. The importance of acceptance cannot be overly stressed. In one way or another practically every ground rule says one thing: accept one another. When you model acceptance of students, they will learn how to be accepting. Each individual in the group is important and deserves a turn to speak if he or she wishes to take it. Equal opportunity to become involved should be given to everyone in the group.

Members should be reinforced equally for their contributions. There are many reasons why a teacher may become more enthused over what one student shares than another. The response may be more on target, reflect more depth, be more entertaining, be philosophically more in keeping with one's own point of view, and so on. However, students need to be given equal recognition for their contributions, even if the contribution is to listen silently throughout the session.

In most of the sessions, plan to take a turn and address the topic, too. Students usually appreciate it very much and learn a great deal when their teachers, counselors, and other adults are willing to tell about their own experiences, thoughts, and feelings. In this way you let your students know that you acknowledge your own humanness.

Does everyone have to take a turn? No. Students may choose to skip their turns. If the group becomes a pressure situation in which the members are coerced in any way to speak, it will become an unsafe place where participants are not comfortable. Meaningful discussion is unlikely in such an atmosphere. By allowing students to make this choice, you are showing them that you accept their right to remain silent if that is what they choose to do.

As you begin the groups, it's important to remember that it's not a problem if one or more students decline to speak. If you are imperturbable and accepting when this happens, you let them know you are offering them an opportunity to experience something you think is valuable, or at least worth a try, and not attempting to force them to talk. You, as a leader, should not feel compelled to share a personal experience in every session, either. However, if you decline to speak in most of the sessions, this may have an inhibiting effect on the students' willingness to share.

Since these sessions will take place online it works best to simply have the students raise their hands when they wish to speak. This approach can also work in a live classroom setting.

Sometimes a silence occurs during a session. Don't feel you have to jump in every time someone stops talking. During silences students have an opportunity to think about what they would like to share or to contemplate an important idea they've heard. A general rule of thumb is to allow silence to the point that you observe group discomfort. At that point move on. Do not switch to another topic. To do so implies you will not be satisfied until the students speak. If you change to another topic, you are telling them you didn't really mean it when you said they didn't have to take a turn if they didn't want to.

If you are bothered about students who attend a number of sessions and still do not share verbally, reevaluate what you consider to be involvement. Participation does not necessarily mean talking. Students who do not speak are listening and learning.

How can I encourage effective listening? The Sharing Circle is a time (and place) for students and teachers to strengthen the habit of listening by doing it over and over again. No one was born knowing how to listen effectively to others. It is a skill like any other that gets better as it is practiced. After a few sessions, the students become keenly aware of the necessity to listen, and most students respond by expecting it of one another.

In these Sharing Circles, listening is defined as the respectful focusing of attention on individual speakers. It eschews interruptions of any kind. When you lead a session listen and encourage listening in the students by (1) focusing your attention on the person who is speaking, (2) being receptive to what the speaker is saying (not mentally planning your next remark), and (3) recognizing the speakers when they finish speaking, either verbally ("Thanks, Shirley") or nonverbally (a nod and a smile).

To encourage effective listening in the students, reinforce them by letting them know you have noticed they were listening to each other and you appreciate it.

How can I ensure the students get equal time? When group members share the time equally, they demonstrate their acceptance of the notion that everyone's contribution is of equal importance. It is not uncommon to have at least one dominator in a group. This person is usually totally unaware that by continuing to talk he or she is taking time from others who are less assertive. An important social skill is knowing how you affect others in a group and when dominating a group is inappropriate behavior.

Be very clear with the students about the purpose of this ground rule. Tell them at the outset how much time there is. When it is your turn, always limit your own contribution. If someone goes on and on, do intervene (dominators need to know what they are doing), but do so as gently and respectfully as you can.

What are some examples of put-downs? Put-downs convey the message, "You are not okay as you are." Some put-downs are deliberate, but many are made unknowingly. Both kinds are undesirable because they destroy the atmosphere of acceptance and disrupt the flow of sharing and discussion. Typical put-downs include:

- over questioning.
- statements that have the effect of teaching or preaching
- advice giving
- one-upsmanship
- criticism, disapproval, or objections
- sarcasm
- statements or questions of disbelief

How can I deal with put-downs? There are two major ways for dealing with put-downs: preventing them from occurring and intervening when they do.

Going over the rules with the students at the beginning of each session, particularly in the earliest sessions, is a helpful preventive technique. Another is to reinforce the students when they adhere to the rule. Be sure to use non-patronizing, non-evaluative language.

Unacceptable behavior should be stopped the moment it is recognized by the teacher. When you become aware that a put-down is occurring, do whatever you ordinarily do to stop destructive behavior. If one student gives another an unasked-for bit of advice, say for example, "Jane, please give Alicia a chance to tell her story." To a student who interrupts say, "Ed, it's Sally's turn." In most cases the fewer words, the better—students automatically tune out messages delivered as lectures.

How can I keep students from gossiping? Periodically remind students that using names and sharing embarrassing information is not acceptable. Urge the students to relate personally to one another, but not to tell intimate details of their lives. Also remind students that what is shared in the session stays in the session. There is no gossiping either in or out of the group.

What should the leader do during the discussion question phase? Conduct this part of the process as an open forum, giving students the opportunity to discuss a variety of ideas and accept those that make sense to them. Don't impose your opinions on the students, or allow the students to impose theirs on one another. Ask open-ended questions, encourage higher-level thinking, contribute your own ideas when appropriate, and act as a facilitator.

In Conclusion: The Two Most Important Things to Remember

No matter what happens in a Sharing Circle session, the following two elements are the most critcal:

1. **Everyone gets a turn.**
2. **Everyone who takes a turn gets listened to with respect.**

What does it mean to get a turn? Imagine a pie divided into as many pieces as there are people in the group. Telling the students that everyone gets a turn, whether they want to take it or not, is like telling them that each one gets a piece of the pie. Some students may not want their piece right away, but they know it's there to take when they do want it. As the teacher or counselor, you must protect this shared ownership. Getting a turn not only represents a chance to talk, it is an assurance that every member of the group has a "space" that no one else will violate.

When students take their turn, they will be listened to. There will be no attempt by anyone to manipulate what a student is offering. That is, the student will not be probed, interrupted, interpreted, analyzed, put-down, joked-at, advised, preached to, and so on. To "listen to" is to respectfully focus attention on the speaker and to let the speaker know that you have heard what he or she has said.

In the final analysis, the only way that a Sharing Circle can be evaluated is against these two criteria. Thus, if only two students choose to speak, but are listened to—even if they don't say very "deep" or "meaningful" things—the discussion group can be considered a success.

ACTIVITIES

How My Life Has Changed Because of the Pandemic

This first topic provides you and the students with an opportunity to acknowledge the impact the COVID19 Pandemic has had on the world's human population while also enabling all of you to identify and share how it has affected you personally. Through this process students are helped to understand that they are not alone in experiencing uncomfortable stressors. It also gives them a chance to share their personal feelings about how it has uniquely affected each of them. Doing so makes it clear to students that everyone has a right to their own thoughts and feelings while learning how others are managing their lives during a stressful time.

Begin the session by introducing the topic then elaborate on the topic in your own words by saying something like this:

"We all know how this pandemic has affected the entire world. It has brought huge difficulties of many different types for all humans. Today's topic, however, is all about you. Think about specific ways in which your own personal life has changed because of it and how you honestly feel about these changes. When you are ready to speak just raise your hand. We will listen respectfully to what you have to say."

(Note: Being the first to respond to this initial topic is a good idea so you can model how to state your own issues and feelings in a calm and honest manner).

Culminate the sharing phase by asking these and/or your own discussion questions to help the students reflect on their learning:

1. *What similarities did you notice in the changes in our lives that we shared?*

2. *What were some of the differences between us in the changes in our lives that we shared?*

3. *Now let's look at how these changes make us feel. Let's see how many feelings we can remember that were mentioned?*

Close the session by thanking the students for their participation and for speaking honestly and listening respectfully.

What I Like About Distance Learning

This topic allows you and the students to acknowledge the "pros" of distance learning (the next one allows all of you to acknowledge the "cons"). Similar to the prior Sharing Circle, this one gives students the chance to hear other students' thoughts and feelings and to share their own. Noting similarities and differences between themselves and others leads to understanding and acceptance of others and oneself.

Begin the session by introducing the topic then elaborate on the topic in your own words by saying something like this:

"With the quarantine in force we find ourselves involved in 'distance learning,' a big change from the way we used to learn by going to school. Distance learning all by itself may have some drawbacks which we will discuss in our next Sharing Circle but, for now, let's focus on the positives. Think for a minute about what you like about it, and why--how you feel about what you like. When you're ready to speak let me know."

Culminate the sharing phase by asking these and/or your own discussion questions to help the students reflect on their learning:

1. *Was there an aspect or two about distance learning that all of us liked?*

2. *What differences did you notice in what we liked about distance learning?*

3. *What were some of the feelings we brought up?*

Close the session by thanking the students for their participation and for speaking honestly and listening respectfully.

What I Don't Like About Distance Learning

This topic is the "flip side" of the former one because it allows you and the students to acknowledge the "cons" of distance learning. Once again this Sharing Circle gives all of you the chance to hear others' thoughts and feelings and to share your own. Noting similarities and differences between themselves and others continues to foster understanding and acceptance of others and oneself. This topic also demonstrates that honestly and calmly stating negative factors and feelings is okay.

Begin the session by introducing the topic then elaborate on the topic in your own words by saying something like this:

"In our last sharing circle we talked about what we like about distance learning. Today we will have the chance to tell each other what we don't like about it and why --how you feel about what you don't like. Think it over for a minute and when you're ready to speak let me know."

Culminate the sharing phase by asking these and/or your own discussion questions to help the students reflect on their learning:

1. *Was there an aspect or two about distance learning that all of us dislike?*
2. *What differences between us did you notice in what we don't like about distance learning?*
3. *What were some of the feelings we brought up?*

Close the session by thanking the students for their participation and for speaking honestly and listening respectfully.

What I Miss Most About Being in School

This topic allows you and the students to reflect on the benefits of learning in the physical presence of others and what all of you may likely miss about it. Sharing disappointments with others who are accepting and kind can cause students to feel less isolated. The students are also given the opportunity to give and receive empathy—something we all need from each other to some extent during a time of physical distancing.

Once again the similarities and differences in different people are addressed with this topic. It is acceptable that some of us are not as socially oriented as others.

Begin the session by introducing the topic then elaborate on the topic in your own words by saying something like this:

"When we learned together in school, we did not foresee this quarantine coming. It was such an abrupt change in our lives. Give the topic a minute's thought and then share with us what you miss most now that we have to stay away from each other physically. Tell us what you miss and why. Add how the things you miss made you feel then and how you feel now without them."

Culminate the sharing phase by asking these and/or your own discussion questions to help the students reflect on their learning:

1. What similarities and differences did you notice in the statements we made?

2. As we have seen some of us enjoy the company of other people more than others do. Is that okay?

3. Did you find out something about someone that you didn't know before?

Close the session by thanking the students for their participation and for speaking honestly and listening respectfully.

Someone (or Something) at Home That Helps Me Feel Okay

This topic provides you and the students with the opportunity to share personal means by which all of you find comfort during an uncomfortable time. This process in itself may provide further comfort. It may also give students ideas for feeling better when isolation becomes depressing.

Begin by introducing the topic then elaborate on the topic in your own words by saying something like this:

"Being cut off so much from the activities we used to enjoy with other people can get pretty depressing for many of us. Probably everyone has a particularly hard time with isolation especially if it means missing an event they really wanted to participate in. It's when those particular disappointments occur that it really helps if there is someone at home who knows how you feel and can help you feel better. Sometimes it's a thing like a favorite stuffed animal or a computer game that you can turn to that helps. If you would like to tell us who or what makes you feel okay, we will be pleased to listen. While you share your thoughts on this topic name the feelings you have about isolation and in what ways someone or something helps you feel better."

Culminate the sharing phase by asking these and/or your own discussion questions to help the students reflect on their learning:

1. *What sorts of feelings did you notice that we mentioned when we talked about isolation and about how someone or something improves things for us?"*
2. *Did you get any ideas for who or what might make you feel better when you are feeling cut off from activities you wish you could participate in?"*

Close the session by thanking the students for their participation and for speaking honestly and listening respectfully.

What's Stressing Me Out and How I Handle It

When our normal daily routines and expectations are radically changed as ours have been due to the COVID19 pandemic, distress (generally referred to as "stress") will understandably occur. This topic allows you and the students another chance to express disappointments as the former topic did. Being more general in nature it gives all of you the opportunity to identify and discuss other stressors related to the pandemic or not. The second part of the topic—"How I Handle It"—is even more important because it places an emphasis on the necessity to *manage* difficulties and *oneself* in the face of those difficulties. This topic also allows all of you to share ways to do it.

Begin the session by introducing the topic then elaborate on the topic in your own words by saying something like this:

"No doubt about it, this pandemic has caused all of us stress—a lot of different kinds of stress. Sometimes it's really stressful just to see other people being stressed. Stress can seem contagious but it doesn't have to be. Notice that this topic has two parts so when you think for a bit about it go beyond what's stressing you out (that's probably the easy part) to how you handle it. Probably the best way to think about it is how you manage yourself during this tough time. See if you can give us a good example of how you overcome your stress so it doesn't get the best of you."

Culminate the sharing phase by asking these and/or your own discussion questions to help the students reflect on their learning:

1. *What similarities and differences did you notice in the sorts of stressors we mentioned?*
2. *Did you hear a good idea from someone for managing yourself when you are dealing with a difficult situation?*

Close the session by thanking the students for their participation and for speaking honestly and listening respectfully.

EXTEND THE LEARNING

Mindful Breathing – Deep breathing is a research-backed method of calming down when stressed or anxious. Teach your students belly breathing, a simple deep breathing exercise that can be done anywhere.

While sitting in front of their computers, ask the students to put all distractions away and to get comfortable. If they would like to close their eyes, they may do so. Read the following directions in a manner that will allow them to experience the sensation of deep breathing while following your instructions.

"Inhale through your nose, while slowly counting to four... Exhale through your mouth while slowly counting to six. Focus on your stomach expanding during the inhale and contracting on the exhale. Feel your body relaxing." (Repeat the directions for breathing in and out enough times so that the students actually get to feel themselves relaxing).

After the experience of deep breathing talk about the value of being able to do deep breathing anytime they find they are stressed or anxious, and that it is a good idea to simply practice deep breathing on a regular basis as a way to give themselves calming benefits all day long.

Words That Help Me Feel Safe and Secure

Language has an enormously powerful effect on the human psyche. Beyond transmitting information, words affect motivation, mood and emotion in multitudinous ways. This Sharing Circle enables you and the students to individually share words from a variety of sources that have an encouraging, comforting and inspiring effect during this difficult period. It also helps the students understand that it isn't helpful to focus on words that threaten feelings of safety and security.

Begin by introducing the topic then elaborate on the topic in your own words by saying something like this:

"The meanings of words we hear, read, speak and think affect us! Words have a huge influence on us. Think about words said directly to you, or words in a movie script, or words you read in a book, or even words you say out loud to someone or that you say in your head to yourself. They are powerful! During a time like this when we are physically cut off from each other it's important for us to be our own best friends by focusing our attention on words that are helpful. We also do ourselves a favor by not listening to, or reading, or saying, or even thinking words that bring us down. In this Sharing Circle you are invited to share some words that you may have heard someone say, or read, or even said yourself to someone or to yourself—words that help you feel safe and secure."

Culminate the sharing phase by asking these and/or your own discussion questions to help the students reflect on their learning:

1. *During a difficult time like this pandemic how important is it for people, especially young people, to focus on words that encourage and comfort them?*
2. *What were some words shared that helped <u>you</u> feel safe and secure?*
3. *Did anyone realize that you may have been listening to, reading, saying or thinking some words that are not helpful?*

Close the session by thanking the students for their participation and for speaking honestly and listening respectfully.

My Hopeful Visions for the Future

During difficult circumstances hope has been a sustaining force for humanity. This Sharing Circle offers you and the students the opportunity to share your personal visions for a better future.

Begin by introducing the topic then elaborate on the topic in your own words by saying something like this:

"While we have been in this state of social distancing and hearing about the tragic effects of the Corona Virus, I keep hoping that it will end soon. I'm sure you have similar hopes. In this Sharing Circle our focus is on what we hope the future <u>will look like.</u> Take a minute to think about what you can see in your mind's eye when things finally take a turn for the better. When will that happen? What will it be like to be physically closer to other people? What about group events? What about changes at home, school, restaurants, church and parties? If you choose to take a turn give us some details about one or two of your hopeful visions for the future and how you think you will feel if your visions come true."

Culminate the sharing phase by asking these and/or your own discussion questions to help the students reflect on their learning:

1. *Do you think this topic helps us realize that the pandemic won't last forever?*
2. *Why is it helpful for us to share the hopeful visions we have for the future?*

Close the session by thanking the students for their participation and for speaking honestly and listening respectfully.

At this time you might say something like this*: "It is my hopeful vision for each one of you to do more than just survive this tough time but to love life and yourselves more than ever starting this very moment."*

My Favorite Place

The first eight Sharing Circle topics in this book spoke directly to the pandemic and the personal issues and feelings that it fosters in all of us. These next topics provide a more general introduction to the Sharing Circle process while providing discussions that help all participants to get to know each other on a personal and meaningful level.

Begin the session by introducing the topic then elaborate on the topic in your own words by saying something like this:

"Today we will be talking about good feelings again by thinking about a particular place where we like to be because we are usually happy when we are there. Your favorite place could be a far away vacation spot or in your own room surrounded by things you love. It can be anyplace near or far. Describe your favorite place and what you see, hear, smell, etc. around you when you are there. Then describe how you feel when you are there."

Culminate the sharing phase by asking these and/or your own discussion questions to help the students reflect on their learning: the sharing phase by asking these and/or your own questions:

1. *What were some of the similarities that you noticed in the places that we told about?*
2. *What were some similarities in the feelings that we described?*
3. *Does talking about a favorite place bring the good feeling a person has when they are there back to the present time? Why do you think that happens?*
4. *How do your surroundings affect your mood? ...Your thoughts?*

Close the session by thanking the students for their participation and for speaking honestly and listening respectfully.

A Time When I Felt Happy

Today's self-awareness topic helps the students express themselves on a very simple subject that is uplifting. It is always a positive experience for people to talk about times when they experienced contentment and joy.

Begin the session by introducing the topic then elaborate on the topic in your own words by saying something like this:

"Remember a time when you were feeling happy. What was it that brought about your happy feeling? Maybe someone did something especially nice for you that you liked. Maybe you were in a special place and felt full of joy and positive energy, or maybe you had just accomplished something that you worked hard to achieve. It could have been a holiday or vacation you were enjoying with your family. There are many things that bring happy feelings. Think of something you would like to share and tell us about it."

Culminate the sharing phase by asking these and/or your own discussion questions to help the students reflect on their learning: *Did you notice anything about what someone said that reminded you of what someone else said*

1. *In what ways were their feelings similar?*
2. *How did just thinking about your happy memory make you feel?*
3. *Why is it good for us to tell each other when we feel happy?*

Close the session by thanking the students for their participation and for speaking honestly and listening respectfully.

EXTEND THE LEARNING:

The Art of Happiness – Direct the students to gather any art materials they have at home. Ask them to draw a picture completing the statement: Happiness is… (This can be written in the chat box). Let them know it doesn't have to be anything big and momentous but it can be as simple as eating dessert first, hitting a home run, or playing with a kitten. The statement that they think of should be something that for each of them would produce happy feelings. Ask them to illustrate their statements with their art materials. Provide a time now, or later, when they can share their happiness statements and art.

One of My Favorite Possessions

Most people have a number of possessions that are particularly significant to them in some way. Today the students will have the opportunity to tell each other about one thing that they possess that they treasure. In the process they examine the values they hold that make the item special

---

Begin the session by introducing the topic then elaborate on the topic in your own words by saying something like this:

"Think about something that is your very own that you like very much. Maybe you've had it since you were very young or you got it more recently. Someone you care about very much may have given it to you, or you may have done extra chores to earn enough money to but it. It could be anything at all that you would like to tell us about. Describe what makes it special to you and how you feel when you hold it or use it or look at it."

Culminate the sharing phase by asking these and/or your own discussion questions to help the students reflect on their learning:

1. *Everyone who took a turn told about a favorite possession, so in that way we were the same. In what ways were we different (possessions or feelings)?*

2. *Do you think it's important for people to have favorite possessions? Why or why not?*

3. *How do your values help you decide which of your possessions are favorites?*

Close the session by thanking the students for their participation and for speaking honestly and listening respectfully.

EXTEND THE LEARNING

Announce the topic the day before and let the students know that if they actually have their favorite possession at home with them they can bring their item to the group so everyone can see it on Zoom while they talk about it.

My Favorite Game

By informing one another of such things as their favorite games and how they feel when they play them or observe them being played, the students are not only becoming more aware of their own and each other's preferences, but also that each person reacts to the external world in their own unique way.

Begin the session by introducing the topic then elaborate on the topic in your own words by saying something like this:

"Think about a game that you enjoy very much. It could be a game you like to play with others or it could be one that you participate in as a spectator. Maybe it's a physical game that is played outdoors or a board game that can be played indoors in a more quiet setting. There are many different games that people play and we generally like more than one, but for today tell us about one of your favorite games and why you enjoy it so much."

Culminate the sharing phase by asking these and/or your own discussion questions to help the students reflect on their learning: the sharing phase by asking these and/or your own questions:

1. *Did everyone who spoke have a favorite game?*

2. *What were the similarities and differences that you may have noticed between the games we told you about and/or how we felt as we played them?*

3. *Why do you think people of all ages like games either to play themselves or to watch others play?*

4. *Did someone else share something about their favorite game that now makes you want to play it or watch it?*

Close the session by thanking the students for their participation and for speaking honestly and listening respectfully.

My Favorite Movie or TV Show

Most people love to watch an exciting movie, TV show or video. Telling others about what happened in the story and how they reacted to it is generally an invigorating experience.

Begin the session by introducing the topic then elaborate on the topic in your own words by saying something like this:

"Think about a favorite show that you have seen recently and tell us about it. Don't try to tell us the whole plot, just tell about the part that was the most important for you. Focus on how you were feeling as you watched this favorite part."

Sometimes young people will tell about episodes that are generally distasteful to most adults and it is hard for us to keep from disapproving. While you are entitled to your feelings too, it is important that you demonstrate to the students that you accept the feelings that they express as long as they are not inappropriate. *Any judgments on your part will very likely be detrimental to any future sharing of feelings.*

Culminate the sharing phase by asking these and/or your own discussion questions to help the students reflect on their learning:

1. *What were some of the main feeling reactions that were expressed in the group today to the movies and TV shows that we told about?*
2. *If your feeling about a particular show changed after listening to someone else talk about it, tell us which show it was, and what your thoughts are now.*
3. *What can we learn from watching movies, TV and video shows?*

Close the session by thanking the students for their participation and for speaking honestly and listening respectfully.

EXTEND THE LEARNING

Cooperative story telling – Explain to the students that TV shows and movie scripts are often created by groups of people working cooperatively to write it. Explain that you will give them a story prompt and by working cooperatively they will write the story by each of them in turn adding a line or two to the story. Give a prompt such as, *"There once was a young wizard who didn't know how powerful he was..."* Record the story in the chat box as each student adds their own line to the story.

A Time When Something Funny Happened

Most people love to relay humorous stories to one another. By "giving permission" to the students to tell about something funny that happened, you are letting them know that laughter and good feelings in the here-and-now are an acceptable part of a Sharing Circle and of life in general. Laughing is a natural stress reliever, and enjoying good times with others is a powerful bonding experience.

Begin the session by introducing the topic then elaborate on the topic in your own words by saying something like this:

"Think about something funny that you saw or that you were involved in that didn't hurt anyone. Tell us about the funny part. It could have been a pre-planned joke or something that just happened spontaneously. Maybe it was something you said or did, or something you saw or heard that was funny. Tell us what happened, how it made you feel, and how you reacted."

Sometimes the students will tell about something that they did as a younger child and as they look back they see it now as funny. This demonstrates their human capability to look at themselves and even laugh at themselves.

Let the students know that it is as acceptable to laugh in these sessions as it is to tell about their feelings. If you feel amused, laugh with them.

Culminate the sharing phase by asking these and/or your own discussion questions to help the students reflect on their learning: by asking these and/or your own questions:

1. *What is it about a funny moment that makes it funny?*
2. *How do most (or all) of us seem to feel when we are reacting to something funny?*
3. *What are the benefits of having a sense of humor?*

Close the session by thanking the students for their participation and for speaking honestly and listening respectfully.

EXTEND THE LEARNING

The Comedy Show – Announce that the students are going to have an opportunity to create humor by participating in an informal "comedy show." Every student will have a turn being a comedian and the rest of the time will be a member of the audience. As comedians, they can tell jokes, read funny poetry, enact silly skits, sing funny songs, or do comical impersonations. Let them know they can work alone, with a partner, or with a small group to plan their "act." Set time lines for developing their "act" and for the actual performances.

A Favorite Book (or Story)

An enjoyable experience for most people is to relate to others a part of a story that to them is meaningful in some way. Stories also provide an important way for students to see the world from another point of view. This helps foster understanding and empathy for others.

Begin the session by introducing the topic then elaborate on the topic in your own words by saying something like this:

"Think about a book or story (not necessarily a book at school) that you found interesting. It could be any story that you have heard or read. Tell us about the interesting part and how you felt as you read or heard that part. Also think about the characters in the story and tell us how you think they were feeling."

Culminate the sharing phase by asking these and/or your own discussion questions to help the students reflect on their learning:

1. *What feelings did most of us have when we read our favorite stories?*
2. *What were some of the other feelings that were told about in this session?*
3. *If all of us read the same story, do you think we would all get the same feelings?*
4. *Why is it important to understand how the characters in the story feel?*

Close the session by thanking the students for their participation and for speaking honestly and listening respectfully.

EXTEND THE LEARNING

Have the students share a few lines from a favorite story, song, or poem.

Something I Like to Daydream About

Everybody daydreams. Daydreams are about using our imaginations to create situations and experiences that we desire, things we want to do, and places we want to go. Whatever the daydream is about it is an important use of our imaginations. This self-awareness topic helps the students to become aware of the impact daydreams, and using their imaginations can have on their lives.

Begin the session by introducing the topic then elaborate on the topic in your own words by saying something like this:

"Do you have something that you like to daydream about? Maybe it is something you did that you like to remember, or someplace you'd like to go. Perhaps it's a creative idea about something you'd like to make or do or write about someday. Since our daydreams are in our imagination, they can be about anything and can help us better understand what we want to do or accomplish. What is something you like to daydream about? Tell us about it, and how you feel when you are in your daydream."

Culminate the sharing phase by asking these and/or your own discussion questions to help the students reflect on their learning:

1. *In what ways do you think daydreaming and using your imagination help you to be creative?*
2. *What do you think people would be like if they didn't daydream and have powers of imagination?*
3. *What are some of the different kinds of feelings that daydreams we told about give to us?*

Close the session by thanking the students for their participation and for speaking honestly and listening respectfully.

What I Would Do If I Were Made King or Queen of the World for One Day

This is a fun and fanciful topic that allows the students to use their imagination and be creative with their thoughts. Our thoughts can have a powerful influence on how we feel. This feel good topic can help propel the students into a positive mood.

Begin the session by introducing the topic then elaborate on the topic in your own words by saying something like this:

"What would you do it you were made King or Queen of the world for a day? Lets pretend that this could happen. What would you do? Would you travel to a place you have never been before? Would you open Disneyland and Disneyworld to all the children in the country? Would you have homes built for the homeless? Would you want to do something special for your family and friends? Be creative and as wild and imaginative as you wish. There are no limits to this topic."

Culminate the sharing phase by asking these and/or your own discussion questions to help the students reflect on their learning:

1. *What are some of the similarities and differences you noticed in what we shared?*
2. *What kinds of feelings did you experience while imagining being Queen or King?*

Close the session by thanking the students for their participation and for speaking honestly and listening respectfully.

Something That I Think Is Beautiful

The things that we find beautiful in the world give us a great deal of pleasure. It is also pleasurable for most people to tell others about what they find to be beautiful. Exploring our concept of beauty can be illuminating, and hearing about what others consider beautiful increases our understanding of them. This also develops the idea that everyone perceives the world in their own unique way.

Begin the session by introducing the topic then elaborate on the topic in your own words by saying something like this:

"Think about something that to you is beautiful. It could be an entire scene, such as a view from a mountaintop, or the vast expanse of the ocean, or it could be just one object, such as a flower. Maybe it's an animal or a man made object like a car or a special dress. Describe your beautiful object and tell us how you feel as you look at it, or hold it."

Culminate the sharing phase by asking these and/or your own discussion questions to help the students reflect on their learning:

1. *Does everyone see beauty in exactly the same things in exactly the same way?*
2. *Is it okay for people to have different ideas about what is beautiful?*
3. *In what ways does a session like this help us to get to know each other better?*

Close the session by thanking the students for their participation and for speaking honestly and listening respectfully.

EXTEND THE LEARNING

Beautiful Collage – Ask the students to gather old magazines, scissors, glue, and a large piece of cardboard or paper. Suggest they look for pictures of things they find beautiful, then cut and glue them onto the cardboard or paper. Set a time for the students to share their collages

A Smile from Someone Special

A smile is a simple yet dynamically powerful and influential behavior. It is a natural function that we do when we are feeling good. This topic helps students understand the "feel good" nature of a smile to benefit both the giver of the smile and the receiver of the smile

---

Note: Before you begin the session, place your COVID mask on your face and ask the group to see if they can tell when you are smiling. They will be able to because a genuine smile affects one's entire face including the eyes. Discuss this with the students including the idea that when we smile it might feel funny and some people get embarrassed when they smile and they stop themselves. Yet, people are probably the most appealing of all when they are smiling. A smile communicates friendliness and good feelings.

Begin the session by introducing the topic then elaborate on the topic in your own words by saying something like this:

"Do you remember a time when someone special smiled at you? What were the circumstances? What did you do when you were smiled at, and how did it make your feel? When you are ready, tell us about it, and how you felt and what you did."

As the students smile throughout the session, remark to them how good they look when they smile. Expect the normal release which will follow in the form of giggling and laughing.

Culminate the sharing phase by asking these and/or your own discussion questions to help the students reflect on their learning:

1. *How do we benefit when we smile at someone?*
2. *How does the other person benefit when we smile at them?*
3. *All of us are aware of how good it feels when someone who is special to us smiles at us. You know, we are all special people to someone else. Think for a moment of who you are special to. How will it make them feel if you smile at them?*

Close the session by thanking the students for their participation and for speaking honestly and listening respectfully.

EXTEND THE LEARNING

A Smile Poster – Using whatever art materials are available to them have the students create a poster around the theme "Smile". Ask the students to think of a slogan that will encourage people to smile, and then to create a poster adding the words and art that will bring a smile to someone's face. The students can think of their own slogan or some possible suggestions are:

- A smile can brighten your whole day,
- Everyone smiles in the same language,
- Exchange a smile with someone,
- Make someone happy - smile at them.

Set a time to have the students share their posters.

Something I'm Looking Forward To

Today we turn our attention toward the future. Imagining a future event with anticipation can be a motivating force to prepare us for the event or to work at making sure we achieve the desired result.

Begin the session by introducing the topic then elaborate on the topic in your own words by saying something like this:

"Think about something you are looking forward to. It could be anything – playing soccer next spring, going on a trip with your family for the weekend or spending time with a friend this afternoon. Maybe it's a competition of some sort that you are looking forward to. Or just having some quiet time reading your favorite book. As you tell us about what you're looking forward to think about how you feel right now as you talk about it, and also how you think you'll feel when you are doing it?"

Culminate the sharing phase by asking these and/or your own discussion questions to help the students reflect on their learning:

1. *Did our feelings about something in the future seem to be as strong as feelings we have about things in the present and in the past?*
2. *Is it important to have things to look forward to? Why?*
3. *What were some other kinds of feelings besides good feelings that were mentioned (if any)?*
4. *What causes these other feelings (if there were any)?*

Close the session by thanking the students for their participation and for speaking honestly and listening respectfully.

A Rule We Have In My Family

This topic invites the students to talk about the rules in their families and to consider the value of rules to any group or organization of people.

Begin the session by introducing the topic then elaborate on the topic in your own words by saying something like this:

"Families like all other organizations have to establish rules. You probably are glad to have some of the rules, but maybe not so happy about others. Maybe your family has a rule that requires you to finish your chores before spending time with friends. Maybe homework must be completed before TV or video games. Some families have rules about bedtime, having friends over when no adult is home, or keeping your room picked up. Things like fighting or name-calling are usually not allowed. Think about the rules in your family and describe one to us."

Culminate the sharing phase by asking these and/or your own discussion questions to help the students reflect on their learning:

1. *What do you learn from having rules?*
2. *How well do the rules work in your family?*
3. *How would things be different if your family did not have these rules?*
4. *If you have a family some day what rules do you think you will establish?*
5. *Why are rules important in any group or organization of people?*

Close the session by thanking the students for their participation and for speaking honestly and listening respectfully.

One of the Best Times I Ever Had With My Family

Today's topic helps the students to recognize and affirm positive family experiences and the value of cooperative activities in enriching family ties.

Begin the session by introducing the topic then elaborate on the topic in your own words by saying something like this:

"Think about a time when you were with one or more of your family members and you had a particularly enjoyable time together. Maybe it was an outing to an amusement park or the beach, or you took a longer family trip to a special vacation spot. Perhaps you were celebrating a family birthday or maybe you all decided to go to the movies together. Maybe it's a special holiday that your family celebrates in a way that you particularly enjoyed. It can be any type of enjoyable family experience. Tell us what you did with your family, and what made it so special."

Culminate the sharing phase by asking these and/or your own discussion questions to help the students reflect on their learning: by asking these and / or your own questions:

1. *What feelings did you have when you were enjoying your good time with your family?*
2. *How did other members of your family seem to feel?*
3. *What differences in feelings and experiences did you notice among the students who shared in this topic?*
4. *Why is it important to have good times with our families?*

Close the session by thanking the students for their participation and for speaking honestly and listening respectfully.

EXTEND THE LEARNING

Family Trees – Talk about the meaning of the term "family tree." You might want to show a diagram of your own family tree as an example. Explain that one way to learn more about one's cultural heritage, or roots, is to do a family tree. Ask the students to research and to draw their family tree by asking their parents and other family members about their ancestors going as far back as there is knowledge. For any students who want to do additional research into their ancestry encourage them to explore the many free online resources available. Set a time for the students to share their family trees and what they learned about their own cultural background.

Note: Some students may be adopted, in foster care, or live in a non-traditional family setting. Help those students complete a family tree with people who are in their lives. Explain that culture is something we learn from those around us, not something we are born with.

An Important Person In My Life

This topic enables the students to consider the personal qualities and behaviors that are modeled by people who are important in their lives. By identifying these qualities, and their positive effects, the students are better able to internalize these positive qualities in themselves.

Begin the session by introducing the topic then elaborate on the topic in your own words by saying something like this:

"Most of us interact with many people every day. Some are friends, some are relatives, and some are strangers. The people who are important to us have usually contributed something special to our lives. They may look after us, guide us, or teach us. Frequently they share our joys and sorrows. Think about one important person in your life. This person could be a parent, grandparent, teacher, counselor, coach, or friend. Tell us how and why this person is important to you, and how you feel when you are with him or her."

Culminate the sharing phase by asking these and/or your own discussion questions to help the students reflect on their learning: the session by asking these and /or your own questions:

1. *What characteristics did our important people have in common?*
2. *If your important person were no longer available to you how would you manage to get along?*
3. *What is the most important thing you have learned from this person?*
4. *Do you think you can be as important to someone else as your person has been to you? If so, what characteristics would you have to demonstrate?*

Close the session by thanking the students for their participation and for speaking honestly and listening respectfully.

A Way I Show Respect For Others

Respect is an important element of healthy relationships, and this topic helps students to focus on specific behaviors that demonstrate respect for others.

Begin the session by introducing the topic then elaborate on the topic in your own words by saying something like this:

"There are many ways that we can show respect for other people. Tell us about a way that you frequently use. Maybe you remember to say please and thank you, or try never to interrupt others when they're talking, or hold doors when you go through them so they won't swing back and smack the people behind you. Perhaps you try not to say critical things about others, or maybe you listen respectfully to the opinions of people you disagree with. Think about it for a few moments. Tell us what you do that is respectful, and how you learned to do it."

Culminate the sharing phase by asking these and/or your own discussion questions to help the students reflect on their learning: the session by asking these and /or your own questions:

1. *How do you feel about yourself when you show respect for others?*
2. *If you want to be respected, will showing respect for others help? How?*
3. *Should we show respect for people we don't like? Explain.*

Close the session by thanking the students for their participation and for speaking honestly and listening respectfully.

I Have a Friend Who Is Different from Me

This topic asks students to identify specific differences between themselves and their friends. Acknowledging differences between themselves and someone they care about helps to foster respect for differences in race, culture, lifestyle and ability between all people.

Begin the session by introducing the topic then elaborate on the topic in your own words by saying something like this:

"We are all alike in many ways, but we are also different. Today, I want you to think about a friend who is different from you in at least one major way, and to tell us why you like this person so much. Perhaps your friend is of a different race, or has a much larger family, or is a lot older than you. Does your friend speak a different language or eat different kinds of food. Does your friend have a disability that causes their lifestyle to be different from yours? Also tell us what you enjoy about your friend. Does your friend listen to you and share things with you? Do you have something in common like a love of sports, or music or computers? Tell us about your difference and what you like so much about your friend."

Culminate the sharing phase by asking these and/or your own discussion questions to help the students reflect on their learning:

1. *What are some of the ways we differ from our friends?*
2. *How are you enriched by the differences between you and your friend?*
3. *What causes some people to dislike others who are different from them?*
4. *What would our lives be like if we could only make friends with people who are just like we are?*

Close the session by thanking the students for their participation and for speaking honestly and listening respectfully.

How I React When I'm Happy

This topic and the next one deal with the positive emotion of happiness. Then the topic following these deals with the very different emotion of anger. Both are powerful self-awareness topics from which the students consider how each can impact their lives.

Begin the session by introducing the topic then elaborate on the topic in your own words by saying something like this:

"Think back to a recent time when you felt very happy. Picture in your mind what was happening and how you reacted. There are many things that can make us happy and there are also many ways we can react to the happiness we feel. Some of you maybe laughed or squealed or jumped up and down or maybe just smiled. Everyone has their own reaction. Even when we are having similar feelings, we respond in different ways and that's okay. Tell us about what it was that made you happy but most importantly tell us how you reacted."

Culminate the sharing phase by asking these and/or your own discussion questions to help the students reflect on their learning:

1. *We told about different ways we reacted to being happy. How many ways were there in this group?*
2. *Can others tell how you feel just by seeing how you react?*
3. *How does it help us to be aware of how others perceive our actions?*

Close the session by thanking the students for their participation and for speaking honestly and listening respectfully.

How I Made Someone Feel Happy

Today the students will focus on their own behavior. It generally makes us happy if we find that we have effectively made someone else feel happy. And our feelings of effectiveness can be enhanced if we have an opportunity to talk about how we did it. Today the students will be able to do just this.

Begin the session by introducing the topic then elaborate on the topic in your own words by saying something like this:

"Think about a time you made someone happy and describe what you did to make them feel that way. Maybe you helped a new student find a classroom or gave an honest compliment on a friend's appearance. Perhaps you stood up for someone who was being bullied or teased. Or you may have helped an elderly neighbor carry groceries. Maybe you gave a special gift to a friend or relative. There are many ways to make someone happy. Tell us what you did to make someone happy and how you could tell that they felt good?"

Culminate the sharing phase by asking these and/or your own discussion questions to help the students reflect on their learning:

1. *What usually happens to our own feelings when we have successfully made someone else feel happy?*
2. *What sort of planning is required to make someone feel happy?*
3. *What would the world be like if we all spent a little more time helping others feel good?*

Close the session by thanking the students for their participation and for speaking honestly and listening respectfully.

EXTEND THE LEARNING

A Happy List – Explain to the students that just as they are able to help make someone else happy they can also do things to help make themselves happy. Talk about the benefits of gratitude and focusing on the "bright side of life". Encourage the students to take a few minutes each day to write down something that makes them happy or that they feel grateful for. Remind them that it doesn't matter how small it is. It can be as simple as a comfy pair of shoes, a sunny day, a good friend, or a loved pet. Tell them they can keep a daily journal or even writing on a piece of paper and keeping the paper in a jar works. The important thing is to write daily and reflect on their happy thoughts, and to re-read their happy list whenever they need a pick-me-up.

A Time I Managed My Anger

This important topic enables the students to consider the importance of self- control and the use of effective strategies when they are angry. It also allows them to consider the role self-talk plays in "coaching" themselves to acknowledge their feelings about upsetting situations and what would be the best ways to act so no one gets hurt including them.

Begin the session by stating the topic then elaborate on the topic in your own words by saying something like this:

"We all become angry at times when upsetting things happen. Sometimes the way people respond just makes things worse--they mismanage their anger, which is very easy to do. But anger can be managed and even lead to a good outcome at times. Think about a time when you became angry and you were able to manage it in some way. Please don't mention the names of any of the people who were involved in the incident. It will be interesting for us to hear about these situations and how you talked with yourself helpfully, controlled yourself, and managed your anger."

Note: You may wish to take your turn first in order to model an appropriate response by relating an incident that you would feel comfortable telling the students about and how you responded with self-control and skillful handling. If you tell them how your anger felt at first and what you might have done if you had not controlled yourself, your story will be realistic and of keen interest. Elaborate by telling them how you told yourself not to do anything until you calmed down and thought things over with your right mind. Finally tell them what you planned to do and how it worked out when you did your plan.

Culminate the sharing phase by asking these and/or your own discussion questions to help the students reflect on their learning:

1. *Did you find yourself feeling empathy for each other as we told about the situations that upset us?*
2. *What if we hadn't used self-control or acted in helpful ways in the situations we shared? What do you think would have happened?*

3. *How important is self-control in managing anger? What about what we say to ourselves at these times?*

4. *Did you get a good idea today for managing anger?*

Close the session by thanking the students for their participation and for speaking honestly and listening respectfully.

EXTEND THE LEARNING

STOP and Stay in Control – Teach your students to remember the acronym STOP whenever they feel their anger or stress level rising.

 S=Stop what your doing.

 T=Take several deep breaths.

 O=Observe, without judging, what you're feeling and thinking.

 P=Proceed with your day in a calm and in-control manner.

Point out that this simple exercise will help them calm down in the moment but also helps to retrain their automatic response to anger and stress, so they stay calmer and more in control in future situations.

It Was Difficult, But I Controlled Myself

This self-management topic allows students to explore times in their lives when their ability to use rational self control overruled the need to react impulsively and, therefore, reinforce their awareness and ability to manage impulses.

Begin the session by introducing the topic then elaborate on the topic in your own words by saying something like this:

"See if you can remember a time when you didn't want to, but you controlled yourself. You may have been about to react strongly to some situation without giving your behavior much thought, but were able to gain control of yourself. It might have been a time when someone else said or did something that was very upsetting, but you didn't let it get to you. Maybe you felt you were being treated unfairly or perhaps it was something like being left out of an activity or game. Think it over for a minute and remember not to share any names, just the incident when you were able to control yourself."

Culminate the sharing phase by asking these and/or your own discussion questions to help the students reflect on their learning:

1. *How did you feel about yourself when you were able to use self-control?*

2. *Sometimes we make things worse when we say or do something that makes us feel better at the moment. How can we judge when it's best to say or do what we feel like doing, and when its best to use self-control and hold ourselves back?*

3. *What are some of the things we can do to maintain self-control during a difficult time?*

Close the session by thanking the students for their participation and for speaking honestly and listening respectfully.

How I Like to Spend My Free Time

Today the students are given the opportunity to tell each other about what they enjoy doing when the choice is theirs. The students may find commonalities of enjoyable pastimes that they didn't know they shared with others in the class. This is often the basis of new friendships.

Begin the session by introducing the topic then elaborate on the topic in your own words by saying something like this:

"Think about one (or possibly two) things that you like to do in your free time when there is no pressure on you to do anything. Maybe you are an energetic person and you like to play sports or games. Maybe you prefer artistic endeavors like music, dance or art. Or perhaps it is just relaxing – reading, watching TV or spending time with friends. Tell us what it is that you like to do when the choice is entirely your own."

Culminate the sharing phase by asking these and/or your own discussion questions to help the students reflect on their learning:

1. *Do all of us seem to like having free time for doing the things we enjoy?*
2. *Do we all enjoy doing the same things?*
3. *Do we enjoy them for the very same reason and in the very same way? (For those who mentioned liking to do the same things.)*
4. *Why is it important to have free time?*

Close the session by thanking the students for their participation and for speaking honestly and listening respectfully.

EXTEND THE LEARNING

My Perfect Day – Ask the students to write a story about a perfect day in their life starting with getting up in the morning and ending when they go to bed at night. What are the things they will be doing all day long that would make it a perfect day? If they can do anything they want with no obligations or commitments what would they do? The day is just for them to do exactly as they want. Set a later date to share the stories.

An Adventure I Had

This is a topic that young people generally love to talk about and are often able to relate detailed accounts. It is used here to help students verbalize feelings and describe emotional experiences. It also helps them identify interests related to things they enjoy and to learn about the adventures and interests of others.

Begin the session by introducing the topic then elaborate on the topic in your own words by saying something like this:

"Think about some kind of an adventure you have had. It could be anything that you did, or were involved in, that made you feel good. It may have been an overnight camping trip, your first ride in an airplane, or a time when you spent the night at a friend's house. It might have been a once-in-a-lifetime kind of adventure or something you get to repeat. Think about the adventure you want to tell us about and then take your turn."

Culminate the sharing phase by asking these and/or your own discussion questions to help the students reflect on their learning:

1. How can listening to someone talk about their adventure help you to get to know them better?
2. Why do people have different ideas about what makes an adventure fun?
3. Is it important to have adventures in our lives?
4. Did you hear about someone else's adventure that makes you want to have a similar adventure someday?
5. What do you think it means when people say, "Life is an adventure"?

Close the session by thanking the students for their participation and for speaking honestly and listening respectfully.

My Favorite Musical Group

Almost all students enjoy some kind of music and like to discuss their favorites. The emphasis today will be on how they respond behaviorally to their favorite music when they hear it.

Begin the session by introducing the topic then elaborate on the topic in your own words by saying something like this:

"Do you have a favorite musician, singer, singing group or band? Describe the music that you like. Then tell us how you feel when you listen to it and how you react to it. When you hear your favorite music or musician, do you sit still and listen, or do you want to get up and move to the music. Think about your favorite music and describe the music that you like, how you feel as you listen to it and how you generally respond to it."

Culminate the sharing phase by asking these and/or your own discussion questions to help the students reflect on their learning:

1. *What were some of the differences that you may have noticed in the preferences we have in musical groups?*
2. *What were some of the different ways that we respond to our favorite music?*
3. *Did you notice any similarities?*

Close the session by thanking the students for their participation and for speaking honestly and listening respectfully.

EXTEND THE LEARNING

Extend the enjoyment of this Sharing Circle with this assignment: "Prepare a sample of what you like best from your favorite musical group. It could be one half minute of the music you could play for us or a portion of the lyrics you could read to us on (state the date/time for these presentations)."

A Hero or Heroine I Admire

Today's topic has the students think about people they admire and the admirable qualities inherent in those people. Through this discussion the students get to consider how people demonstrate admirable and beneficial qualities to others, and the benefits to society of people with admirable qualities worthy of emulation.

Begin the session by introducing the topic then elaborate on the topic in your own words by saying something like this:

"As you look back at the people you know or have heard about or read about that have done admirable and courageous things, who is it that stands out in your mind? It could be a real life person or a fictional character. If it's a real person it could be someone you know personally, like a member of your family or a friend. Or it might be someone you know of who stood up for people's rights, or one who had the courage to say or do something that no one else would do. Your chosen hero or heroine may be someone you've studied in school, or learned about elsewhere. Tell us who your hero or heroine is, and what that person did to earn your admiration."

Culminate the sharing phase by asking these and/or your own discussion questions to help the students reflect on their learning:

1. *How are our heroes and heroines alike? How are they different?*
2. *Why is it important to have people to look up to and admire?*
3. *What can our heroes and heroines teach us?*
4. *What character traits does your hero or heroine demonstrate that you can try to cultivate in your own life?*

Close the session by thanking the students for their participation and for speaking honestly and listening respectfully.

If I Could Do Anything I Wanted

Today the students will have the opportunity to use their imaginations to think of actions that they would enjoy if they could do anything they wanted.

Begin the session by introducing the topic then elaborate on the topic in your own words by saying something like this:

"Think of something that you would like to do if you could do anything you wanted that wouldn't bother or hurt anyone else. It might be something that seems very unlikely to ever happen or something that might happen. Tell us about what it would be and how you think you would feel if you could actually do the thing you are imagining doing."

Discussions of why they have not done these things, or the likelihood that they ever will, are not necessarily relevant.

Culminate the sharing phase by asking these and/or your own discussion questions to help the students reflect on their learning:

1. *Would all of us choose to do the same thing if we could do anything that we wanted to do?*

2. *Did some of us expect to have similar feelings if we could do anything we wanted to do, even though the actions might have been different?*

3. *What role does imagination play when you are creating or inventing something?*

Close the session by thanking the students for their participation and for speaking honestly and listening respectfully.

What People Need from Each Other In Order to Be Good Friends

This topic asks the students to think about their own friendships and identify personal qualities and ways of interacting that strengthen them. They can then start to develop a generalized understanding of the ingredients of healthy relationships

---

Begin the session by introducing the topic then elaborate on the topic in your own words by saying something like this:

"We all have experienced the feeling of being in a place where we feel good. Often, one of the main reasons that we feel good is that we also feel safe. Can you think of a place where you generally experience a feeling of safety? Maybe it's in a particular location like your home or the home of a relative or friend, or maybe you feel it with a certain person. The safety you feel could be with a person or from the place you are in. Is there some place where you feel safe and comfortable? When you're ready tell us about it."

Culminate the sharing phase by asking these and/or your own discussion questions to help the students reflect on their learning:

1. *Do you think people need to trust each other in order to be good friends? Why or why not?*
2. *What ingredients did most of us think were needed in a good friendship?*
3. *What makes a friendship last a long time?*

Close the session by thanking the students for their participation and for speaking honestly and listening respectfully.

A Person I Feel Safe With

The best friendships are between people who trust each other. They trust each other because they are careful not to hurt each other. They make it safe for each other to "be themselves" when they are together. Today's topic goes hand-in-hand with, "A Place Where I Feel Safe," which follows it. Today, the students will concentrate on the same concepts of safty and security via a close look at certain human behaviors.

Begin the session by introducing the topic then elaborate on the topic in your own words by saying something like this:

"Do you know someone with whom you feel safe? . . . Someone you can trust not to hurt you – your body, or your feelings? Tell us about the person and in what way you feel safe with him or her. Think about their behavior toward you and the kinds of things they say to you to make you feel safe."

Culminate the sharing phase by asking these and/or your own discussion questions to help the students reflect on their learning:

1. *What are some of the main things we shared that made us feel safe with someone?*
2. *How does the person you feel safe with treat you?*
3. *In most cases, were the people we told about accepting of our feelings?*
4. *How do people we feel safe with teach us important lessons?*

Close the session by thanking the students for their participation and for speaking honestly and listening respectfully.

A Place Where I Feel Safe

By discussing this topic the students will focus on their own personal experiences and feelings of safety and security. This helps them identify components of a secure, trust-building environment and to understand the value such a place has in their lives.

Begin the session by introducing the topic then elaborate on the topic in your own words by saying something like this:

"We all have experienced the feeling of being in a place where we feel good. Often, one of the main reasons that we feel good is that we also feel safe. Can you think of a place where you generally experience a feeling of safety? Maybe it's in a particular location like your home or the home of a relative or friend, or maybe you feel it with a certain person. The safety you feel could be with a person or from the place you are in. Is there some place where you feel safe and comfortable? When you're ready tell us about it."

Culminate the sharing phase by asking these and/or your own discussion questions to help the students reflect on their learning:

1. *Do you think it's important for everyone to have a place where they feel safe?*
2. *What things could make a place feel unsafe?*
3. *Does this Sharing Circle group feel like a safe place?*
4. *What do we try to remember to do in a Sharing Circle session to make it a safe place? (Discuss how in the Sharing Circle listening and accepting the feelings of others in the group can make it a safe place. If you accept someone's feelings, you are accepting them. If you reject their feelings, you are rejecting them).*

Close the session by thanking the students for their participation and for speaking honestly and listening respectfully.

EXTEND THE LEARNING

Guided Imagery- Explain to the students that they can bring the good feelings of their safe place into their life anytime they want through the simple mental exercise of guided imagery. Tell them that you will take them through the process of how to do this so they can do it whenever they want. Ask the students to find a comfortable position and close their eyes as they listen to you read some relaxing mental suggestions. As you read pause long enough after each suggestion to allow them to recreate the experience in their minds. In a quietly audible voice read the following guided imagery:

> *"Relax and breathe slowly and deeply through your nose and exhale fully through your mouth…breathe slowly in and slowly out…feel yourself becoming relaxed and calm…In your imagination see your safe place ahead of you in the distance… walk toward your safe place…see yourself getting closer and closer…Now walk into your safe place and feel its peaceful, inviting, relaxing feelings envelope you…look around and notice what you see…What is above your head…beneath your feet…on either side of you?..Is there anyone there to greet you?...Listen to the sounds around you…what do you smell?... Notice the temperature… Feel relaxation and peace gently wash over you…This is your special place, nothing can harm you … you can let go of all tension…you are relaxed, you are safe, you are comfortable…Remember you can come here anytime you wish. The good feelings of your safe place are available to you any time you want… Take a deep breath and turn around and leave your safe place going back the way you came…When you are ready, open your eyes and take a few moments to enjoy the relaxation in your mind and body."*

Someone Who Trusts Me

Today the students will be given the opportunity to focus their attention on how it feels to have someone trust them and how trust can develop between people. Some may not have been aware, up till now, when they stop to think about it, that there is someone who trusts them. For some of the students, the "someone" who trusts them maybe be an animal. (In the case of those students who cannot think of anyone who trusts them, this will be an important session too.)

Begin the session by introducing the topic then elaborate on the topic in your own words by saying something like this:

"Think of a person who trusts you and tell us how you earned that trust. Did this person always trust you or did you have to earn their trust? Maybe you showed that you could be trusted to take care of a younger brother or sister or that you always remember to feed your dog his dinner. Maybe you earned someone's trust by always telling the truth even when it got you in trouble. Tell us what it is you do to show someone that you can be trusted and how it feels to be trusted by this person."

Culminate the sharing phase by asking these and/or your own discussion questions to help the students reflect on their learning:

1. *For most (or all) of us, what was the feeling we had about having someone trust us?*
2. *How do you know they trust you?*
3. *Do you usually trust people who trust you?*
4. *What kind of things can destroy trust?*
5. *Why is trust important in relationships?*

Close the session by thanking the students for their participation and for speaking honestly and listening respectfully.

Someone I Don't Trust Very Much

Today we look closely at the opposite side of the coin, which will continue to bring the issues involved in trust and relationships into sharp focus. The best friendships are between people who trust each other. They trust each other because they are careful not to hurt each other.

Begin the session by introducing the topic then elaborate on the topic in your own words by saying something like this:

"Is there someone who you don't trust very much? Don't tell us the person's name if it's someone you know personally, just tell us what the person does that makes it hard for you to trust him or her. Perhaps the person you think of is in a story you read or a character you've seen in the media. If you take a turn, briefly tell about what kinds of things the person does (or did) that causes (or caused) you not to trust them very much."

Note: This is a topic that is negative in tone, so it would probably be best if you took your turn first in order to demonstrate to the students that it is okay to discuss it. Point out to the students at the outset that today it is particularly important that they remember not to mention names if they talk about someone they know personally.

It is likely that some will refrain from speaking today. Many may need to just listen. Treat the topic in a very matter-of-fact way. Be sure to demonstrate by your behavior to the students who speak that their feelings of not trusting someone are acceptable. To those who do not wish to speak, demonstrate that their wish to just listen is acceptable.

Culminate the sharing phase by asking these and/or your own discussion questions to help the students reflect on their learning:

1. *What kinds of things do the people that we don't trust very much do?*
2. *If you want people to trust you, how do you think you should treat them?*

Close the session by thanking the students for their participation and for speaking honestly and listening respectfully.

How I Show Someone That They Can Trust Me

Today the students will focus their attention directly on the critical area of how people behave when they want someone's trust. Reflecting on their own behavior and listening to others report on theirs, the students may become more capable of seeing the link between their behavior and how they are reacted to by others. For some it may be the first time for them to directly consider the idea that if they want someone to trust them, there may be one or more things they could do to earn that trust.

Begin the session by introducing the topic then elaborate on the topic in your own words by saying something like this:

"Think about a time when you wanted someone to trust you. Maybe it was a parent or other relative, or a friend, teacher, or coach. Perhaps you were hoping that this person would give you a special privilege or trust you to take care of something that belonged to them. Describe the situation and tell us how you convinced the other person that you could be trusted. Did you simply talk the person into trusting you or did you have to demonstrate your reliability?"

Culminate the sharing phase by asking these and/or your own discussion questions to help the students reflect on their learning:

1. *If you let someone know that you trust them, do you think it might help them to trust you?*

2. *If you have earned someone's trust, does that trust automatically last for as long as you know them?*

3. *Why is trust important to good relationships?*

Close the session by thanking the students for their participation and for speaking honestly and listening respectfully.

EXTEND THE LEARNING

Elements of Trust - There have been several topics dealing with different elements of trust and the students have considered this character trait from many angles. A good summary to these topics would be to conduct a think-pair-share to make a list of the elements of trustworthiness. Follow the usual format of a think-pair-share. First having the students individually think of the elements, then work in pairs via Zoom to share and expand their thinking. Finally, invite the students to report their lists to the whole group.

Discuss the benefits to individuals and society when people demonstrate the traits of trust listed by the students.

A Time When I Trusted Myself, or I Knew I Could Do It

Whenever we experience a situation in which we prove to ourselves that we are capable, our capacity to trust ourselves more in the future expands. It is a very positive experience overall. By sharing a time when they trusted themselves, the students are given the opportunity to reinforce these positive feelings.

Begin the session by introducing the topic then elaborate on the topic in your own words by saying something like this:

"Think about a time when you were pleased with yourself because you did something you were sure you could do. There are many times in our lives when we have to ask others for help or advice. But there are other times when we have to trust our own ability to solve our problem. Take a moment to think about a time when you trusted your own skills, knowledge or experience. Maybe you trusted yourself to solve some difficult math problems, or maybe it was trusting yourself to step up to the microphone to sing a solo in the school play, or you score the goal that gives your soccer team the title. It could be anything big or small that you trusted yourself to do. Tell us about what happened, and how you felt when you found out that you were right to trust yourself?"

Culminate the sharing phase by asking these and/or your own discussion questions to help the students reflect on their learning:

1. *Can a person learn to trust him or herself more?*

2. *What methods can you use to learn to trust yourself more?*

3. *What are some circumstances under which you should always seek help from someone else?*

Close the session by thanking the students for their participation and for speaking honestly and listening respectfully.

I Taught Myself Something

In this session the students will consider the idea that learning often happens when people make the personal effort to learn something or to "teach themselves." It is our objective today, to give the students the opportunity to tell about how they taught themselves something (or learned something all by themselves). By discussing such important events as these, the students may at some level, consider the idea that the teacher is not responsible for "teaching" them everything that's worth learning. They may also see how they are in a position to influence their own lives with respect to the skills and knowledge that they are motivated to achieve.

Begin the session by introducing the topic then elaborate on the topic in your own words by saying something like this:

"Tell us about something that you taught to yourself. It could be anything that you can think of. Maybe you helped yourself to learn how to read, or understand a math problem, or to ride a bike or skateboard, or how to draw a picture of a certain kind of animal. The struggles that we often go through to learn things may not feel good at the time, but it's usually worth it to keep struggling because of the feelings of accomplishment we get. Think about what you would like to share. It doesn't matter how big or small it is. We would like to know what it is you taught yourself and how you feel about it now."

Culminate the sharing phase by asking these and/or your own discussion questions to help the students reflect on their learning:

1. *What is the feeling that most of us seem to have about teaching ourselves something?*
2. *How does it feel now to know that you can teach yourself to do things?*
3. *Is it only up to the teacher to teach us everything?*

Close the session by thanking the students for their participation and for speaking honestly and listening respectfully.

The Way I Learn Best

Besides giving the students the opportunity to consider and tell about the ways that they learn, you as their teacher are in a position to gain valuable and interesting information about their learning styles.

Begin the session by stating the topic then discuss the difference between visual (seeing), auditory (hearing), and tactile/kinesthetic (touching and moving) learning styles. Also spend a little time talking about other conditions different people need for optimal learning like quiet or soft music, working alone or with others, a clean organized workspace etc. Then elaborate on the topic in your own words by saying something like this:

"Think about some of the things that you have learned easily and well. How did you do it? Did you need to see it, hear it, or touch it? Did you need to be with others to really get it, or did you learn it best by your self? Is there a particular place you can go to study that helps you to learn? Tell us about what kind of learner you are and the ways that you learn best."

Culminate the sharing phase by asking these and/or your own discussion questions to help the students reflect on their learning:

1. *Do all of us learn best in the very same way?*
2. *How does it help us to be aware of the ways we learn best?*
3. *What can be done now to make learning easier for you?*

Close the session by thanking the students for their participation and for speaking honestly and listening respectfully.

EXTEND THE LEARNING

Plan to Learn – Write this ancient proverb in the chat box:

"If I Plan to Learn, I Must Learn to Plan."

Ask the students what this means to them. Have the students share their ideas. Then ask: *"What plan can you put in place to help yourself learn? Think about what you learned from this Sharing Circle regarding how you learn best. Then think of a plan you can put in place to assist your learning."* Have the students respond to this question in pairs and then have them each write up their own learning plan. Set a date for the students to share how their plan is working with their partner and with you. Get ideas on how you can further assist them with their learning plans.

Something I Learned That Was Enjoyable

It is the objective of this activity to help students focus on the idea that much of the learning that goes on in their lives can be enjoyable and rewarding.

Begin the session by introducing the topic then elaborate on the topic in your own words by saying something like this:

"Learning is going on all the time for all of us, both in and out of school. Think about something that you learned that you liked, something that is enjoyable for you and that you get a lot of pleasure in learning about. Maybe you enjoyed learning to play tennis or a musical instrument, or perhaps you enjoyed learning to speak a second language or solve difficult math problems. It could have been something you learned at school, but not necessarily. Whatever it is that you find enjoyable to learn about tell us what it is when you're ready."

Culminate the sharing phase by asking these and/or your own discussion questions to help the students reflect on their learning:

1. *What similarities did you notice in the kinds of things we enjoyed learning?*
2. *What can make a learning situation enjoyable?*
3. *Is it possible that learning can produce good feelings?*

Close the session by thanking the students for their participation and for speaking honestly and listening respectfully.

Something I'm Learning About Now That is Hard

Today's session should follow, "Something I learned that was Enjoyable," because it relates to the other side of the coin. Sometimes learning is difficult. By discussing the things they find difficult, the students will begin to realize that everyone has certain learning problems. Thus, each student realizes that there is nothing strange or bad about them if a certain subject area or task does not seem enjoyable or interesting and if they have feelings of frustration. Just about everyone has trouble learning something.

Begin the session by introducing the topic then elaborate on the topic in your own words by saying something like this:

"Today, we are going to talk about times when learning gets tough – and it does for all of us now and then. Are there things that you are learning about now either in or out of school that are difficult for you? Maybe you are studying a foreign language and remembering the vocabulary and grammar is tough. Perhaps you are having difficulty with math, or science. Or maybe it's something like learning to be on time, making new friends, or controlling your temper. Practically everything we do involves learning, so difficult learning can occur in almost any area of our lives. If you feel like telling us about what is difficult for you, we would like to hear."

Briefly discuss how everyone seems to have their own unique problem area. Focus on the feelings that were expressed.

Culminate the sharing phase by asking these and/or your own discussion questions to help the students reflect on their learning:

1. *If you have problems learning certain things, are you the only one?*
2. *What similarities did you notice in the kinds of difficulties we are having?*
3. *Does it help to learn something when you are interested in it?*
4. *Do you have any ideas about where you can go to get help with what you're learning that is hard?*

Close the session by thanking the students for their participation and for speaking honestly and listening respectfully.

A Time When Someone Listened Well to Me

Today the students will be focusing on the critical element of listening in effective communication. By recalling, and telling about, a time when someone listened well to them, the students will begin to connect the idea of good listening with the positive feelings that result in the person who was listened to. They will also begin to identify the characteristics of good listeners and to develop awareness of the skills of good listening.

Begin the session by introducing the topic then elaborate on the topic in your own words by saying something like this:

"You may be noticing as we participate in these Sharing Circles, that listening is a must if we want to have good sessions. As you think about it all interactions between people seem to be more positive and comfortable if everyone who is speaking is listened to. Think about a time when you needed, or wanted, to have someone listen to you very much, and they did listen well to you. Tell us about the situation and how it made you feel to be listened to."

Culminate the sharing phase by asking these and/or your own discussion questions to help the students reflect on their learning:

1. *How important do you think it is for people to listen to one another when they are talking to each other?*
2. *How does it make you feel when someone is really listening to you?*
3. *How do you feel when the person you are talking to isn't listening?*
4. *What do you notice the other person is doing that lets you know that you are being listened to?*

Close the session by thanking the students for their participation and for speaking honestly and listening respectfully.

Once When Someone Wouldn't Listen to Me

Today the students will continue to focus their attention on the important element of listening respectfully to one another. In this session they will tell about a time when someone wouldn't listen to them when they needed to be listened to.

Begin the session by introducing the topic then elaborate on the topic in your own words by saying something like this:

"Did you ever need to have someone listen to you very much, but they wouldn't do it? Maybe you wanted to talk to a friend about something that was bothering you but they were too busy to listen. Sometimes when we get into a conflict we want to tell our side of the situation but the other person refuses to listen. Think of a time when something like this happened to you. What was the situation, how did you feel and what did you do. Please don't tell us who the person was, just tell us what happened and how you felt about it."

Culminate the sharing phase by asking these and/or your own discussion questions to help the students reflect on their learning:

1. *What are some of the feelings we get when we want someone to listen to us and they won't do it?*
2. *How do you feel about the person who wouldn't listen to you?*
3. *What can you do to get someone to listen to you?*
4. *How does this make you feel about listening well to others?*

Close the session by thanking the students for their participation and for speaking honestly and listening respectfully.

A Time When I Listened Well to Someone

Today the students will have an opportunity to tell about a time when they listened effectively to another person. By describing their positive behavior, and taking deserved credit for it, the behavior is likely to be reinforced.

Begin the session by introducing the topic then elaborate on the topic in your own words by saying something like this:

"We've been doing a lot of talking and sharing in our groups, and we have also been listening well to one another. If we hadn't been good listeners, our discussions wouldn't have worked. Listening is just as important to communication as talking.

"Can you think of a time when you listened carefully to another person? Perhaps you had a friend who needed to talk about a problem, and you showed you cared by listening. Or maybe it was a situation in which you learned a lot from someone who had interesting and important things to say. Think about times like these, when you used your listening skills, and tell us about one of them."

Culminate the sharing phase by asking these and/or your own discussion questions to help the students reflect on their learning:

1. .How much does it affect another person's feelings if you listen to them?
2. What are some of the ways that people show that they are listening?
3. What are the things you do to show that you are really listening to someone?
4. How do you feel about yourself now as you realize that you are able to be a good listener?

Close the session by thanking the students for their participation and for speaking honestly and listening respectfully.

EXTEND THE LEARNING

A Listening Experiment – Explain to the students that you will be conducting an experiment in what it's like to really listen carefully. Make sure they each have a piece of paper and a pen or pencil. Ask the students to carry out the following directions. Each direction may be repeated.

1. Draw a large perpendicular oval in the center of your paper.
2. Draw 5 small circles running up and down the center of the oval.
3. Draw a circle above the oval making it touch the oval.
4. Draw a triangle above this circle making a flat side touch the top of the circle.
5. Draw a tiny circle above the triangle making it touch the tip of the triangle.
6. Draw a long horizontal oval shape near the top right of the big oval making it touch the oval.
7. Draw a hand on the end of this oval.
8. Draw a long horizontal oval shape near the top left of the big oval making it touch the oval.
9. Draw a hand on the end of this oval.
10. Draw two long oval shapes hanging down from, and touching, the large center oval.
11. Draw big shoes on the ends of these ovals.

When this part is done have the students share their drawings. How many drew a clown? This is a good time for laughter as they compare what they came up with. Follow up with a discussion about how difficult, or easy, it was following directions and the importance of good listening skills.

A Time When We Communicated Without Words

When we stop and think about it, it is surprising how many things, especially feelings, we can communicate to someone without the use of words. Often non-verbal communication can be a very positive experience. Such emotions as love, for example, need more than verbalization to be fully expressed. By the same token, negative sentiment can be readily transmitted through facial expression, gesture, and so on. Effective listening, therefore, requires more than simple attention to words.

Begin the session by introducing the topic then elaborate on the topic in your own words by saying something like this:

"Think about a time when, for some reason, you couldn't talk with someone out loud so the two of you communicated with each other without words. You may have communicated your feelings to each other and maybe you even communicated some kind of a message. Did you use your body or face, or both to communicate? Tell us about what happened and how you were able to communicate without using words."

Culminate the sharing phase by asking these and/or your own discussion questions to help the students reflect on their learning:

1. *How many different ways did we communicate without words?*
2. *How easy, or hard, was it to understand each other without using any words?*
3. *If it is possible to communicate without words, why don't we do it all the time?*

Close the session by thanking the students for their participation and for speaking honestly and listening respectfully.

EXTEND THE LEARNING

The opportunity for the students to learn more about the power of nonverbal communication could occur by showing them a YouTube scene with the sound off. Select one with a number of dramatic elements. Assign the students to carefully observe and take notes on the characters' eye contact, gestures, facial expressions, postures and movements. Also, ask them to write down what they think was going on between the characters and how each one was feeling. Next, ask the students to individually share their specific observations with the group and what they believe was happening in the scene including the feelings of the characters. Play the YouTube scene again, this time with the sound on.

Finally, ask the students, *"How well did you understand what was going on and how the characters were feeling by carefully observing their nonverbal communication?"* Encourage a discussion about how nonverbal communication really communicates very well, maybe sometimes even better than verbal communication.

How I Let Others Know That I Am Interested in What They Say

Today the students will focus on people's behaviors when they are conversing that show they are interested in what the speaker is saying. The prior four topics had the students consider the different aspects of effective and ineffective listening behaviors. Today's topic will focus on the specific behaviors demonstrated by the students when they are really listening effectively to someone else.

Begin the session by introducing the topic then briefly discuss how such things as body posture, the way we look into someone's eyes, the facial expressions that we make, not interrupting and so on, give messages to the people with whom we are talking that tell them whether or not we want to listen to them. Then elaborate further on the topic in your own words by saying something like this:

"When someone is talking to you and you are interested in what they are saying, what specific things do you do to let them know you care about what they are saying? Think about what you do and say and then tell us what they are."

Culminate the sharing phase by asking this and/or your own discussion questions to help the students reflect on their learning:

1. *Let's try to remember the things that we can do to let people know that we are interested in what they are saying. What are they?*

Close the session by thanking the students for their participation and for speaking honestly and listening respectfully.

EXTEND THE LEARNING

As the students list the behaviors of good listening write them in the chat box. Ask the students to also write them down and encourage them to refer to these listening behaviors in the future.

A Name I'd Like to Have

Since our names are one of the most definite things about us it is ironic that we generally have nothing to say about what they should be. Perhaps it is in response to this situation, that most young people enjoy fantasizing that they have another name – one that they pick. A great deal of pleasure usually comes from this session. It is a good way to begin focusing on the concept of identity because in an enjoyable context the students will begin to think about how they are known and how they would like to be known.

Begin the session by stating the topic and then elaborate on the topic in your own words by saying something like this:

"Our names are very personal to each of us and it's a way we identify ourselves to the rest of world. Even though our names are so personal to us they were given to us by someone else and maybe that's why most of us, one time or another, think about a different name we might like to have. Some people have actually changed their names, sometimes going through legal channels to do so. Have you ever thought about what name you would have chosen for yourself, if the choice had been yours? What name would you have picked? Tell us why you picked that name and what the name means to you?"

Culminate the sharing phase by asking these and/or your own discussion questions to help the students reflect on their learning:

1. *Did we all choose the names that we told about for the same reason?*
2. *What were some of the different reasons you noticed?*
3. *How do you think you would feel being known by the name you chose for yourself?*
4. *Why do you think names are so important to people?*

Close the session by thanking the students for their participation and for sharing honestly and listening respectfully.

If I Were an Animal

Today the students will continue to use their abilities to fantasize by making an even more dramatic choice about their identities. Although the concept may at first be startling, most people enjoy imagining what it would be like not to be human at all, but to be an animal of their choice and to tell about how they decided what animal they would be. Through this kind of expression, the teller and listeners are in a unique mind-frame that together they all understand. Enjoyment, and possibly insight, comes from this experience of vivid self-expression.

Begin the session by introducing the topic then elaborate on the topic in your own words by saying something like this:

"If you were not a person, but some animal, what animal would you like to be? Tell us what you think it would be like to be the animal of your choice. Maybe you would like to be a wild animal living in the jungle or forest or maybe an animal like you have living in your home. It can be any kind of animal at all. Tell us what the animal is, how you decided what animal you would be, and how would it feel to be that animal?"

Culminate the sharing phase by asking these and/or your own discussion questions to help the students reflect on their learning:

1. *What similarities and differences did you notice in the animals we named and the feelings we expressed in this session?*
2. *We all used our imaginations to identify an animal we would like to be like. Is it important to be able to imagine things, even if they are not always possible? Why or why not?*
3. *What would be the best thing about being the animal you chose?*

Close the session by thanking the students for their participation and for speaking honestly and listening respectfully.

A Person I'd Like to Be Like

This is another topic that comes close to getting at the heart of the matter of identity. By thinking about someone they admire and respect in some way, the students will focus on what the characteristics and behaviors of that person are. By considering the traits of a role model they are likely to increase their knowledge of what specific attributes go into being who they want to be.

Begin the session by introducing the topic then elaborate on the topic in your own words by saying something like this:

"Think about someone you would like to be like. Do you know an older teenager, a young adult, or an older adult whom you look up to? It might be someone you know personally like a brother, sister, cousin or neighbor. Or it might be someone you have never met like a TV star or sports figure, or maybe it's your favorite hero, or heroine from history. Tell us about the person and the reasons why you would like to be like that person."

Culminate the sharing phase by asking these and/or your own discussion questions to help the students reflect on their learning:

1. What characteristics did our role models have in common?
2. Is it possible to learn how NOT to be from certain models? Explain.
3. What positive attributes does your model demonstrate that you would like to have?

Close the session by thanking the students for their participation and for speaking honestly and listening respectfully.

EXTEND THE LEARNING

Positive Attributes- using the think-pair-share model ask the students to make a list of positive attributes of admirable people. As they consider the traits have them think about people they know and also famous people in the news, sports and entertainment. Culminate with a group list that can also be written in the chat box.

Someone Who Demonstrates a Lot of Courage

This topic has the students identify specific acts of courage and to focus on the value of courageous behaviors. In doing so they will also identify other character traits associated with valor.

Begin the session by introducing the topic then elaborate on the topic in your own words by saying something like this:

"People show courage in many ways. Some people are courageous in the way they handle illness, severe injury or other personal tragedy. Fire fighters who go into burning buildings to rescue people are seen as courageous. Health care workers during the pandemic are seen as courageous. People who spoke out or demonstrated on behalf of civil rights in the U.S. and South Africa, knowing that they might be hurt or jailed for their actions, were courageous. Tell us about someone that you know personally, or have heard about, such as a famous historical figure, who has demonstrated courage."

Culminate the sharing phase by asking these and/or your own discussion questions to help the students reflect on their learning:

1. *How do we feel about people who show courage?*
2. *What other character traits were demonstrated by the courageous people we described?*
3. *What enables people to demonstrate courage?*
4. *What can make it hard sometimes for people to be courageous?*
5. *Why do courageous people often become role models?*
6. *What have you learned from today about how you can show courage?*

Close the session by thanking the students for their participation and for speaking honestly and listening respectfully.

EXTEND THE LEARNING

Have the students do research and then write a short report on the person they identified as demonstrating courage. Set a time for the students to share their reports with the rest of the group. Allow the other students to ask questions after each report has been shared.

A Group I Like Belonging To

An important part in how we identify ourselves has to do with groups to which we belong. Most people join groups that they feel comfortable being a part of and to which they feel a sense of belonging, and with whom they share common interests or goals.

Begin the session by introducing the topic then elaborate on the topic in your own words by saying something like this:

"Think about some group that you belong to that you like. You could tell about some kind of formal club, sports team, or other organization or maybe it's just a neighborhood group of friends that casually get together. Tell us something the group does that you enjoy. And also think about how you contribute to the group and how the group contributes to you."

Culminate the sharing phase by asking these and/or your own discussion questions to help the students reflect on their learning:

1. *Why do you think people join groups, clubs and organizations?*
2. *How can a group let others know they are open to new members?*
3. *How do you feel about belonging to your group?*

Close the session by thanking the students for their participation and for speaking honestly and listening respectfully.

Who I Am Culturally

The discussion of culture is generally important to people of all ages. Students who are members of minority cultures are very aware of who they are. To experience appreciative, respectful listening as they tell about themselves culturally will be a positive experience. Students of the majority culture often do not focus on themselves in this way. A session of this nature then is likely to increase their awareness that they are a member of a cultural group with its own language, custom, music, beliefs, etc., and that everyone in the world is not guided by these same cultural influences.

Begin the session by stating the topic and briefly discussing what culture is and how it influences us before elaborating further by saying something like this:

"First, tell us what your cultural heritage is, which is usually identified by the cultural or national backgrounds of your parents or grandparents. Then think of how you are an individual because of ways your culture has influenced you. Maybe it's seen in things like your choice of clothes, the holidays you celebrate or the food you enjoy at home. Next, tell the group something you are happy to have in your life because of these cultural influences. Maybe you're pleased and proud to be bilingual, or maybe it's the special feeling you get when you hear the music of your culture. Perhaps it's the excitement of your holiday celebrations or the peacefulness of religious rituals. Take some time to think about all these things. Then take your turn to tell us about who you are culturally and the positive effects your culture has on you."

Culminate the sharing phase by asking these and/or your own discussion questions to help the students reflect on their learning:

1. Why is it a good thing for us to be proud of our cultural heritage?

2. How does it help us to understand each other better when we know something about our cultural backgrounds?

3. Did you learn anything new about someone during this session?

Close the session by thanking the students for their participation and for speaking honestly and listening respectfully.

EXTEND THE LEARNING

Family Interviews –Have the students talk to their parents, grandparents or other family members about where they were born. Ask them to discuss how, and why, they came to the U.S. from another country, or another region in the U.S. Ask them to find out such things as: What were the reasons for, and hopes underlying the move? What is it like to leave one's home and go where they really don't know what to expect? What was the same in both places, and what was different? What problems did they encounter in moving to a new place?

Using the information the students learned from their family interviews assign pairs of students to create interview questions and then to enact video interviews with each other. One student is the interviewer and the other is the immigrant being interviewed. These can be shared with the group via the Internet, or if using a hybrid model they can take place when students meet in class.

A Special Occasion or Holiday That Relates to My Culture

This topic continues the exploration of the students' different cultural backgrounds by acknowledging and appreciating their meaningful traditions.

Begin the session by introducing the topic then elaborate on the topic in your own words by saying something like this:

"Some special occasions or holidays are referred to as 'rites of passage' Events like the christening of a baby, a baptism, a bat or bar mitzvah, a wedding or a funeral mark a person's passage from one stage of life to another. Not every event of this nature is enjoyable, of course, but even funerals offer a kind of comfort to family members.

"Many of the values and attitudes handed down from one generation to another last a long time because they are a traditional part of a certain way of life; they stand for something important and treasured in the culture. Some examples are the Fourth of July, Cinco de Mayo, Easter or Passover. You probably have many special traditions or holidays in your culture. Think about it and pick one that you would like to share with the rest of us."

Culminate the sharing phase by asking these and/or your own discussion questions to help the students reflect on their learning:

1. *What do holidays and rites of passage do for people?*
2. *Why is it important to honor cultural traditions?*
3. *How do you feel about doing traditional things that your ancestors did?*
4. *Did you learn anything new about another culture that you didn't know before this Sharing Circle?*

Close the session by thanking the students for their participation and for speaking honestly and listening respectfully.

Something I Like That Is Part of Another Culture

Continuing with the discussions on culture this topic has the students focus on a culture other than their own. Through identifying something they like and enjoy from another culture it helps to get them to consider the benefits of living in a culturally diverse nation.

Begin the session by introducing the topic then elaborate on the topic in your own words by saying something like this:

"Today we'll talk about things we appreciate from other cultures. Maybe you appreciate a type of music or dance that originated in another culture. Maybe you like the sound of another language like Italian or German or Spanish. It could be the ethnic food that you enjoy like Thai or Chinese or Greek. It could be the traditional holidays of another culture or the spiritual tradition of Native Americans. Describe the thing that you like and tell about any special feelings that go along with it."

Culminate the sharing phase by asking these and/or your own discussion questions to help the students reflect on their learning:

1. *What similarities and differences did you notice in the things we shared?*
2. *If something from your culture or cultural heritage was mentioned, how did that cause you to feel?*
3. *What are some of the many ways we benefit by living in a culturally diverse culture?*

Close the session by thanking the students for their participation and for speaking honestly and listening respectfully.

EXTEND THE LEARNING

Throughout the year find unique and special ways to celebrate cultural events and holidays that are important to your students.

I Helped Someone Who Wanted My Help

This topic is the first of five topics dealing with the subject of helping. In today's session, we will focus on the good feelings that can result from appropriate helping behaviors, before we begin to examine the complexities. In this session the students will focus on the idea that helping and being helped can be a very satisfying experience for everyone concerned.

Begin the session by introducing the topic then elaborate on the topic in your own words by saying something like this:

"Think about a time when you helped someone who wanted your help. Maybe a classmate needed help with a math problem and you took the time to explain it. Perhaps your Dad wanted help working in the yard, or maybe you saw an elderly neighbor struggling with grocery bags and you helped carry them in. Tell us about your situation, how it made you feel to be helpful, and how you think the other person felt when you helped them."

Culminate the sharing phase by asking these and/or your own discussion questions to help the students reflect on their learning:

1. *Who usually feels good when one person helps another?*
2. *What does it take to be a good helper?*

Close the session by thanking the students for their participation and for speaking honestly and listening respectfully.

Someone Helped Me When I Wanted to Be Helped

This session explores the opposite side of the coin from the previous session. Now the students will think about how it feels to be the person who has been helped when they wanted it, by remembering a time when this happened to them.

Begin the session by introducing the topic then elaborate on the topic in your own words by saying something like this:

"In our last session we talked about a time when you helped someone. Today you're going to talk about a time when you were the person who wanted some help and received it from someone else. You could have received help from a friend or relative or even from someone you didn't know. Remember that help can be as simple as carrying grocery bags or something that requires more time and effort. Tell us about what happened when you got some help and how you felt as the person on the receiving end of the help."

Culminate the sharing phase by asking these and/or your own discussion questions to help the students reflect on their learning:

1. *How did the people who helped us seem to feel about getting a chance to be helpful?*
2. *How did we let these people who helped us know that we appreciated their help.?*

Close the session by thanking the students for their participation and for speaking honestly and listening respectfully.

I Got Some Help I Didn't Want

This seems to happen to everyone to some degree. Young people are especially sensitive to what they can and cannot do and often resent attempts on the part of someone else to do something for them that they have learned to do for themselves. In many cases when students are struggling with a task, they are going through important, self-stimulated learning experiences, and need to be involved in the struggle. There is a fine line in these cases, when someone is struggling with a task, when doing something for them may be very helpful or not helpful at all.

Begin the session by stating the topic and then briefly discuss the ideas stated above with the students before elaborating further by saying something like this:

"Have you ever received some help you didn't want? Tell us about what happened and how you felt at the time. Also let us know if your 'helper' seemed to realize that you did not want their help."

Culminate the sharing phase by asking these and/or your own discussion questions to help the students reflect on their learning:

1. *Is there anything wrong with feeling annoyed if someone helps you when you don't want it?*

2. *Why do you think people sometimes try to help someone when the person doesn't want help?*

3. *What do you think is the best thing to do when someone starts to help you and you'd rather do it yourself?*

Close the session by thanking the students for their participation and for speaking honestly and listening respectfully.

I Asked for Help When I Needed It

Today the students will discuss how they felt and what happened when they asked for help when they needed it. Sometimes it takes courage for us to admit being in need of help. It also takes courage because we might be refused, which would probably make us feel bad. For those reasons, people are often hesitant to ask for the help they need.

Begin the session by stating the topic and then briefly discuss the ideas stated above with the students before elaborating further by saying something like this:

"Tell us about a time when you asked for help when you needed it. What were you feeling when you asked for help and how did you feel about the outcome? For some, the outcome may have been a very positive experience, but for others, negative. Either outcome is always possible depending on who is involved and the circumstances. If you would like to share tell us about a time you asked for help, what happened, and how you felt about the outcome."

Culminate the sharing phase by asking these and/or your own discussion questions to help the students reflect on their learning:

1. *Sometimes it's hard to ask for help. How does it make you feel when someone you ask for help doesn't want to help you?*

2. *If this happens, is it easy to ask the next time, even if it is someone else? Why or why not?*

3. *If someone asks you for help, what would you do?*

Close the session by thanking the students for their participation and for speaking honestly and listening respectfully.

I Helped Someone Even Though I Didn't Feel Like It

This topic continues with the discussion of helping and is the last of five. In the previous topic, we talked about how we take risks when we ask for help. We might receive it, or we might be refused, which would probably make us feel bad. In this topic the students are asked to consider what they would do if they were asked to help even though they didn't feel like it. This makes them think about their own behaviors in relation to the needs and request of others.

Begin the session by introducing the topic then elaborate on the topic in your own words by saying something like this:

"Have you ever been asked to help when you didn't want to, but you did it anyway? Tell us about the situation and what happened. Three things to think about are: How did you feel at first? How did the other person seem to be feeling? And how did you feel after you finished helping?"

Note: Expect diversity. Some of the students may have helped because they didn't want the person to feel bad and after helping, they felt good about themselves. Others may have felt that they had better do it, or be punished in some way, and then felt resentful. Discuss how circumstances, and the way we are asked to help, can make a big difference.

Culminate the sharing phase by asking these and/or your own discussion questions to help the students reflect on their learning:

1. *How did most of us feel after helping someone even if we didn't want to do it at first?*
2. *What are some of the things that you may have learned from these sessions about helping?*

Close the session by thanking the students for their participation and for speaking honestly and listening respectfully.

A Way in Which I'm Responsible

This topic asks students to describe responsible behaviors in which they regularly engage. In the process they develop an awareness of the values of taking responsibility and following through on commitments"

Begin the session by introducing the topic then elaborate on the topic in your own words by saying something like this:

"Think of a responsibility that you accept and carry out. It may be a chore that you regularly do around your house. Perhaps your responsibility is to do your homework every night before bed. Maybe your responsibility is to get yourself up every morning and off to school on time. Maybe now your responsibility is to get online in time for your distance instruction. Do you earn and save money? Do you feed and water your dog or cat everyday. These are all ways of being responsible. Share with us one way that you are demonstrating that you are a responsible person."

Culminate the sharing phase by asking these and/or your own discussion questions to help the students reflect on their learning:

1. *What did you learn about hearing about the responsible things other students do?*
2. *Why do you think it's important to have responsibilities?*
3. *How does being a responsible person make you feel about yourself?*

Close the session by thanking the students for their participation and for speaking honestly and listening respectfully.

Something I Worked Hard At

The objective for this session is to give the students a chance to describe something that they put a lot of effort into, and to be acknowledged for that effort. Acknowledging effort, not just intelligence and talent, is a significant way to develop persistence and a strong work ethic.

Begin the session by introducing the topic then elaborate on the topic in your own words by saying something like this:

"Think about a time when you worked very hard at some kind of job or project. It could have been a class project at school or maybe you helped a parent do a project at home. Maybe you worked very hard at learning to play a musical instrument or developing the skill needed to make the team. It can be anything at all that you put real effort into achieving or learning. Tell us what it was and how you did it."

Culminate the sharing phase by asking these and/or your own discussion questions to help the students reflect on their learning:

1. *How do you feel now about all the hard work you put into getting what you wanted?*
2. *While you were working hard did that time always feel good?*
3. *How do most of us feel now about looking back on something that we worked hard at?*
4. *In what ways did your hard work pay off?*

Close the session by thanking the students for their participation and for speaking honestly and listening respectfully.

Something I Do Well That I Like to Do

In the session today the students will validate themselves by verbally "owning" something that they do well. They will also be given the opportunity, via the content of the session, to gain increased awareness of their personal competencies, interests and preferences, and those of their classmates

---

Begin the session by introducing the topic then elaborate on the topic in your own words by saying something like this:

"When we think carefully to ourselves, everyone of us knows about something that we do well. Today, we will encourage each other to speak very positively about ourselves in this session. It can be anything at all from dancing to reading to cooking to being a good friend. It might seem like this is a topic that asks you to brag about yourself a little, and that's okay. You are not boasting or comparing yourself to someone else. And you are not putting anyone else down. You are simply describing what you know you can do well."

Culminate the sharing phase by asking these and/or your own discussion questions to help the students reflect on their learning:

1. *Is it generally easy for us to say positive things about ourselves in a group? Why or why not?*

2. *Why do you think it is important to be able to recognize the things that we do well?*

3. *What kinds of feelings do you get when you acknowledge to yourself that you do something well?*

Close the session by thanking the students for their participation and for speaking honestly and listening respectfully.

Something I Did (or Made) That I'm Proud Of

Today the students will have another opportunity to increase their awareness of their own capabilities by identifying personal accomplishments. This topic is similar to "Something I Do Well That I Like To Do," but the focus is more directly on the pride they feel in their accomplishment.

Begin the session by introducing the topic then elaborate on the topic in your own words by saying something like this:

"We've all done something, or made something, which we are proud of. Think of an example from your life to share today. It can be an accomplishment from when you were a young child or something more recent. Maybe helping someone who needed help made you feel proud. Or you made something like a delicious cake or fixed something that was broken. Maybe the thing that comes to mind makes you proud because other people thought well of you for doing it, or perhaps your accomplishment is something no one knows about except you. Tell us about something you're proud of."

Culminate the sharing phase by asking these and/or your own discussion questions to help the students reflect on their learning:

1. *Are all of us the same in that we all like to feel proud of ourselves for getting a job done well?*
2. *How important is it for people to feel proud of themselves?*
3. *How does pride in ourselves help us continue to accomplish things?*

Close the session by thanking the students for their participation and for speaking honestly and listening respectfully.

Something That I Want to Do (or Make) Someday That I Haven't Done Yet

Today's session is of a very open-ended nature. It offers the students the opportunity to look into the future and to think about something that they presently wish for, or plan to do that may actually happen some day. They may go as far into the future in responding as they wish.

Begin the session by introducing the topic then elaborate on the topic in your own words by saying something like this:

"Is there some kind of job or project that you would like to do someday, or something that you would like to make, that you haven't done yet? It could be what you would like to do when you are an adult, or that you would like to do in a few months or years, or possibly even something that you are looking forward to doing in the next few days. It can be something big and long term, or short and simple. It doesn't matter what it is, just share something that you would like to do or make someday."

Culminate the sharing phase by asking these and/or your own discussion questions to help the students reflect on their learning:

1. *How far into the future did we go when we thought about what we wanted to do (or make) someday that we haven't done yet?*
2. *Is it easier to think about something that you want to do (or make) in the next few days than it is to think of something you want to do (or make) in years, or even as an adult?*
3. *How do you think you will feel when you are actually doing, or making, the thing that you want?*
4. *How can setting goals help you get what you want?*

Close the session by thanking the students for their participation and for speaking honestly and listening respectfully.

Something Worth Saving Money For

Today the students will discuss some of the things that they believe are valuable enough to save their money for and how they feel about waiting and saving for something.

Begin the session by introducing the topic then elaborate on the topic in your own words by saying something like this:

"If you had some money and you were going to save it, what do you think is valuable enough to save for? Maybe you are saving your money for something now. In either case, think about the thing in your life that is worth saving for. It might be a new pair of shoes, a cell phone or computer, or maybe a college education? It doesn't matter how much money something will cost. What we're looking for is what is important enough to you to actually save for."

Do not allow the discussion to center on how much money each child has, rather help them focus on things that they consider to be worth saving for, regardless of how much they've got to save.

Culminate the sharing phase by asking these and/or your own discussion questions to help the students reflect on their learning:

1. *How do you feel about waiting for something as you save for it?*
2. *How do you think it will feel when you have saved enough to get the thing you want?*
3. *Do you think that you should always save every bit of money that you have?*
4. *Should you spend it all? Why or why not?*
5. *Why is saving money sometimes so difficult?*

Close the session by thanking the students for their participation and for speaking honestly and listening respectfully.

EXTEND THE LEARNING

Enrich this Sharing Circle by asking the students to draw a picture of themselves enjoying the thing or situation they think is worth saving money for. Ask them to write a caption below the drawing—the more clever, the better. Set a time/date for sharing their drawings and captions with the group. When the sharing occurs ask the students if they have any questions for the student who has just shown his or her drawing and caption.

Something That I Like to Do Now That Could Relate to My Job When I'm An Adult

Today the students will have the opportunity to see how some of the things that they enjoy doing now might possibly relate to their career choice. This topic encourages them to assess their personal aptitudes, interests and abilities relative to future career possibilities. This is an important notion. The more a young person becomes aware of the kinds of things that they enjoy doing, the more likely they are to find a job in the future that coincides with their preferences.

Begin the session by introducing the topic then elaborate on the topic in your own words by saying something like this:

"We all have skills and talents that we use every day. Maybe you are good at solving math problems, or organizing your study materials. Do you like to build or repair things? Do you draw, sing, play a musical instrument or dance well? Do you like working with people or do you enjoy working on the computer? All of these skills and talents, and many more, are useful in certain jobs. Think about something that you like to do now that could in some way relate to the kind of job you could have when you are an adult. Tell us about it."

Note: Be very sure to remain perfectly accepting in this session. If a student names some kind of occupation that you feel is unlikely for them, be very careful that you in no way reflect this back. People who now hold responsible and rewarding jobs first imagined themselves doing so at some earlier time in their lives. For this reason, this session is likely to be an important one for many of the students.

Culminate the sharing phase by asking these and/or your own discussion questions to help the students reflect on their learning:

1. *Is it too early to start thinking about the kinds of jobs we like?*
2. *How can knowledge of your interests and skills assist you in planning a career direction?*
3. *How do you think it would feel to have a job where you were able to do something you really enjoyed doing?*

Close the session by thanking the students for their participation and for speaking honestly and listening respectfully.

EXTEND THE LEARNING

Interviewing and Reporting – Ask the students to conduct two interviews with people who have jobs that seem interesting to them. Provide these questions for the students to ask in their interviews:

1. Name of person interviewed
2. Job title
3. Company/Organization
4. How long have you held this job?
5. Why did you choose this career?
6. What other jobs have you had along the path to this job?
7. What did you study in school that helps you in this career?
8. How much schooling have you had?
9. What special training did you have for this job?

Have the students give oral reports about what they learned from the job interviews and if there was any specific information that they can use as they start thinking about their future career choice. They can also report on their reactions to the interview process itself.

What I Value In a Friend

By discussing the things that they value in people who they call their friends, the students will, in this session, be focusing directly on various qualities and behaviors. By doing so, they will gain information, which may increase their awareness of what kinds of qualities and behaviors are generally seen as being desirable in a friend.

Begin the session by introducing the topic then elaborate on the topic in your own words by saying something like this:

"Think about the things that you feel are important for friends to do for each other and the kinds of qualities that you think a good friend should have. What do you and your friends say and do to make your friendships work. What qualities do you think are important in a friend? Do you value honesty, loyalty, listening, common interests? Tell us about some of the things that you have thought of that are of value in your friendships."

Culminate the sharing phase by asking these and/or your own discussion questions to help the students reflect on their learning:

1. *What were some of the main things that were mentioned in this session about the qualities we value in friends?*

2. *If you want your friend to have these qualities, does this mean that these would be good qualities for you to have too?*

Close the session by thanking the students for their participation and for speaking honestly and listening respectfully.

One of the Best Times I Ever Had With a Friend

Today the students will have an opportunity to share enjoyable experiences that they have had with their friends, which in itself is a positive experience. They will also learn what kinds of things others their age like to do.

Begin the session by introducing the topic then elaborate on the topic in your own words by saying something like this:

"Think about a time when you were with a friend and you were having a wonderful time together. Tell us how you felt and how your friend seemed to feel."

Culminate the sharing phase by asking these and/or your own discussion questions to help the students reflect on their learning:

1. *Did all of us get exactly the same feelings in exactly the same ways when we had good times with our friends?*
2. *What differences in experiences and feelings did you notice?*
3. *Why is it that with friends good times can be simple – they don't have to involve exciting places and spending lots of money?*

Close the session by thanking the students for their participation and for speaking honestly and listening respectfully.

Something I Never Do When I Want to Make Friends With Someone

In today's session the students will focus their attention on the kinds of behaviors they deliberately avoid when they want someone to like them. By sharing in this way, each student will have an opportunity to gain an increased awareness of ineffective modes of social interaction.

Begin the session by introducing the topic then elaborate on the topic in your own words by saying something like this:

"If you want to make friends with someone, what is something you would never do? Being aware of what turns people off and what makes them like you is difficult sometimes, because people are all so different. But most of us have a pretty good idea of what we don't like, so that's a good place to start. Think about something you would never do when you want to make a friend and what you think might happen if you did do it."

Culminate the sharing phase by asking these and/or your own discussion questions to help the students reflect on their learning:

1. *Did you find yourself thinking about how you would feel if any of the actions we mentioned were done to you?*

2. *How can you recognize the effects of your behavior on others?*

3. *What are some good things to do when you want to make friends?*

Close the session by thanking the students for their participation and for speaking honestly and listening respectfully.

One of the Nicest Things A Friend Ever Did for Me

It is a genuinely heartwarming experience for people to be able to tell others about something nice that someone did for them. Today the students will have an opportunity to do this. Through this kind of discussion they will increase their repertoire of friendly behaviors.

Begin the session by introducing the topic then elaborate on the topic in your own words by saying something like this:

"Think about something that was very nice that a friend did for you. They may have given you something, or they may have asked you to a party, or maybe they said something to you that made you feel very good. Whatever it was, we would like to hear about it and how it made you feel."

Culminate the sharing phase by asking these and/or your own discussion questions to help the students reflect on their learning:

1. *How do you think our friends felt when they did these nice and kind things?*
2. *Did you take note of how we let our friends know we appreciated what they did?*
3. *How can you let a friend know that you appreciate what they have done for you?*

Close the session by thanking the students for their participation and for speaking honestly and listening respectfully.

EXTEND THE LEARNING

Thank you notes - Studies have shown that there are many benefits, both mental and physical to feelings of gratitude. After this Sharing Circle topic a beneficial follow up would be to have the students write a note of thanks to their friend who did something nice for them. Discuss the good feelings thank you notes bring to both parties and the kind of things to say to express gratitude in a thank you note. Even if the notes are not ultimately sent the real benefit comes from the focus on one's feelings of gratitude.

Something Nice That I Did For a Friend

Today the students will take deserved credit for their positive behavior, by telling about something nice they did for a friend.

Begin the session by introducing the topic then elaborate on the topic in your own words by saying something like this:

"In our last Sharing Circle we talked about something nice a friend did for us. Today we're going to give ourselves a pat on the back by talking about our own good deeds. Think about something nice that you did for a friend, and tell us what it was. Keep in mind that many of the kindest things we can do for others doesn't involve money, but involves our time, attention, and understanding. Tell us about the nice thing you did and also, how your friend seemed to feel about what you did."

Culminate the sharing phase by asking these and/or your own discussion questions to help the students reflect on their learning:

1. Why do you think we do nice things for our friends?
2. What similarities did you notice in the feelings we get when we do nice things for our friends?

Why is it important for friends to do nice things for each other once in a while.

Close the session by thanking the students for their participation and for speaking honestly and listening respectfully.

EXTEND THE LEARNING

Friendly Behaviors – Have the students compile a list of positive things that friends do for each other. Think-Pair-Share is a good process for this activity. The idea is to have the students focus directly on the positive behaviors of friendship and understand how to demonstrate them in their own interactions with others.

My Friend (or Friends) Tried to Make Me Do Something I Didn't Want to Do

Today the students will discuss the issue of peer pressure and its effects. By relating this concept to a specific time when one or a group of their peers tried to influence them, the students will have an opportunity to become more aware of how peer pressure operates. Through such a discussion, leading to awareness, it follows that they will also have the opportunity to become more personally in charge of directing their own lives, and less likely to succumb to the will of others.

Begin the session by introducing the topic then elaborate on the topic in your own words by saying something like this:

"Think of a time when you were with one of your friends or a group of friends, and they tried to get you to do something that you didn't want to do. It isn't necessary to tell whether or not they succeeded in getting you to do it, just tell us about what happened and how you felt about it without mentioning any names."

Culminate the sharing phase by asking these and/or your own discussion questions to help the students reflect on their learning:

1. *Do you have to do what your friends want you to do?*
2. *Do your friends have to do what you want them to do?*
3. *When you are trying to get a friend to do something is it harder to convince the friend to do it when you are alone or when you are in a group?*
4. *What did you learn from this topic?*

Close the session by thanking the students for their participation and for speaking honestly and listening respectfully.

I Reached Out to Someone When I Knew They Needed a Friend

Today the students will focus on their power to positively affect the feelings of another person. Our objective in this session is to give them an opportunity to become aware of how potent their friendly instincts and actions are and to see the value in this kind of positive behavior. Through this awareness, it is likely that friendly behavior will be reinforced.

Begin the session by introducing the topic then elaborate on the topic in your own words by saying something like this:

"Think about a time when you knew that someone needed a friend so you did something to show them you wanted to be friends. Tell us what you did and how you did it without naming who it was. You might also mention how the person reacted and how you felt about yourself for reaching out."

Culminate the sharing phase by asking these and/or your own discussion questions to help the students reflect on their learning:

1. *We are finding out in these sessions about the kinds of power that we have. What power did we discuss today?*

2. *How does it make you feel when you need a friend and somebody is friendly to you?*

Close the session by thanking the students for their participation and for speaking honestly and listening respectfully.

When I Was The One Who Needed a Friend

In this session the students will tell about a time when they were the ones who needed someone to show them some care or interest. Everyone at one time or another can be the one to reach out to someone who needs a friend and by the same token we all experience times when we are the ones in need of friendliness.

Begin the session by introducing the topic then elaborate on the topic in your own words by saying something like this:

"In our last session we talked about times we reached out to someone who needed a friend. Today we are looking at this from the other angle. Think about a time when you needed a friend. This happens to us all at times. Maybe you were a new student, or you were feeling bad about something and you wanted someone to reach out to you and be friendly. Tell us about the situation, what happened and how you felt."

Culminate the sharing phase by asking these and/or your own discussion questions to help the students reflect on their learning:

1. *When we have that "I need a friend" feeling, is it a strong feeling for most of us?*

2. *How much will it affect someone if they need a friend and you reach out to them?*

3. *If you need a friend and no one approaches you in a friendly way, what could you do?*

Close the session by thanking the students for their participation and for speaking honestly and listening respectfully.

When My Friend Moved Away

Today's session provides the students with an opportunity to remember old friends who they used to enjoy knowing and to talk about how they felt when these relationships ended. Since it is a part of life that many relationships end in one way or another, a general benefit from this session is derived from allowing the students to discuss this reality together, realizing that separation and loss affects everyone, and that sad feelings are normal. As they respond, expect and accept their sad feelings.

In some instances a student may tell about a relationship that was ended by the death of the person who they enjoyed knowing. Respond sympathetically as you normally would and ask the student how he or she felt and feels now about it. The chance to express grief in a supporting and accepting environment will undoubtedly be appreciated and helps with the healing process)

Begin the session by introducing the topic then elaborate on the topic in your own words by saying something like this:

"Think of a time when a relationship that you enjoyed ended somehow. Maybe your friend moved away or maybe you were the one who moved. Tell us about what happened and how you felt about it."

Culminate the sharing phase by asking these and/or your own discussion questions to help the students reflect on their learning:

1. *How do you feel now as you remember your friend?*
2. *How do you think your friend felt about the separation?*
3. *Does it help to talk with others about sad feelings?*
4. *What are some of the things that you noticed about this session that you would like to mention?*

Close the session by thanking the students for their participation and for speaking honestly and listening respectfully.

Something That Annoys Me

Today the students will have an opportunity to get some of their vexations and frustrations "off their chests." By initially discussing things that annoy them, they will begin this unit with the understanding that everyone becomes bothered at one time or another by something.

This is a particularly valuable session especially for those students who very infrequently express dissatisfaction, for whatever reason. These students will learn that it is okay to express a negative feeling and opinion in certain contexts and the other students may come to see them more realistically.

Begin the session by introducing the topic. Then, briefly discuss how everybody deals with things that bother them and how the people who generally seem to get along well have found reasonable ways to handle their annoyances. Elaborate on the topic in your own words by saying something like this:

"Today we are going to have a chance to talk about things that bother us. Think about something that 'bugs' you and tell the group about it. Be sure not to tell the name of the person, if it is a person, that 'bugs' you."

Culminate the sharing phase by asking these and/or your own discussion questions to help the students reflect on their learning:

1. *What were the similarities that you noticed among this group with respect to the kinds of things that "bug" us?*
2. *What differences did you notice?*
3. *What are some realistic things we could do when these things happen without making the situation worse?*

Close the session by thanking the students for their participation and for speaking honestly and listening respectfully.

A Time When I Was Disappointed

Being disappointed is something children and teens have to deal with often since they are not in a position to acquire, and/or do, everything they would like. This session allows them to gain an important awareness as they share reasonable disappointments and unreasonable fantasies that became calamities when they didn't get what they wanted. It also allows them to think about how people create these responses themselves within their own minds.

Begin the session by introducing the topic then elaborate on the topic in your own words by saying something like this:

"Think about a time when you were disappointed about something. Possibly you wanted to get something and you didn't get it, or you wanted to go somewhere and you didn't get to go. Sometimes we are disappointed in ourselves or in others. Disappointments can be reasonable and unreasonable. When they are reasonable they are just disappointments. When they are unreasonable the person has created a fantasy in his or her mind. When we are being unreasonable we aren't 'grounded' and we think it's a calamity if we don't get what we want. Think of an example in your own life—a reasonable disappointment or an unreasonable calamity. If your story involves other people please don't mention their names."

Culminate the sharing phase by asking this and/or your own discussion questions to help the students reflect on their learning:

1. *Who turns a disappointment into an unreasonable calamity?*
2. *What in this session may have been a good "lesson" for you?*

Close the session by thanking the students for their participation and for speaking honestly and listening respectfully.

A Time I Disappointed Someone

In the previous topic the students discussed how they responded to disappointments which were likely caused by what someone else did or didn't do. Today they are possibly more ready to "own" how they disappointed someone else and to discuss the feelings the other person felt and how they (the students) feel about it now.

Begin the session by introducing the topic then elaborate on the topic in your own words by saying something like this:

"Tell us about a time when you were in a position to do something for someone, or give them something, but you didn't do it causing them to feel disappointed. (It could be that you believed you were doing the right thing and maybe you still see it that way.) Maybe it was yourself you disappointed. If you feel comfortable telling us about it we would appreciate hearing what happened, or didn't happen, how you felt at the time and how you feel about it now?"

Culminate the sharing phase by asking these and/or your own discussion questions to help the students reflect on their learning:

1. *Do you have the power to disappoint people?*
2. *What can you do about someone's disappointment in you?*

Close the session by thanking the students for their participation and for speaking honestly and listening respectfully.

How I Would Solve Somebody Else's Problem

It is always easy for people to figure out solutions to the problems that others have. Today the students will talk about how they were able to see solutions for other people's problems. They will also discuss why it is so easy for us to be able to solve somebody else's problem and so hard for us to solve our own.

Begin the session by introducing the topic then elaborate on the topic in your own words by saying something like this:

"Have you ever known somebody who had a problem when the solution seemed simple to you and you felt like you knew exactly what they needed to do. Think back to how they seemed to feel about their problem and describe what you noticed. Also, if you told the person what you thought they ought to do, tell us how they reacted but please don't tell us who the person was."

Culminate the sharing phase by asking these and/or your own discussion questions to help the students reflect on their learning:

1. *Why do you think it's so easy for someone who doesn't have the problem to know what a good solution might be?*
2. *There are times when we don't really know the best way for others to solve their problems. How can you show them you understand their feelings and that you care?*

Close the session by thanking the students for their participation and for speaking honestly and listening respectfully.

EXTEND THE LEARNING

Giving Advice – Ask the students to imagine that they are the writer of an advice column for the school paper. Tell them that you are going to read them a letter from a student who wants some advice. Then ask them to write a response to the letter after you read it. Have everyone share their response letter. Through this enjoyable and funny activity, help the students understand that problem solving can involve many alternatives and it's important to consider the effects the solutions will have on everyone involved.

Dear AAA Advice Service:

Please help me with my problem. I'm already a teenager and I'm still afraid of the dark. My friends keep inviting me to spend the night with them, but I always say no because I'm afraid that I might start screaming after they turn out the lights.

Why am I still afraid of the dark? What should I do? Please give me some advice.

Sincerely,

Scared E. Katt

A Problem I'm Still Trying to Solve

Today the students will discuss some of the frustrations they may be having with respect to problems they are dealing with at present. This helps them understand that all of us have ongoing unsolved problems. It's normal. This session also allows them to realize that their problems belong to them and other peoples' problems belong to those other people. Taking on other peoples' problems is generally not helpful to anyone. The students will also be given the opportunity to consider ways to show empathy to someone with a problem.

Begin the session by introducing the topic then elaborate on the topic in your own words by saying something like this:

"Think about a problem you have right now that for some reason or other, you haven't been able to solve yet. It might be because you don't have the knowledge or ability to solve it. Everyone has problems like that in their lives. Sometimes the problem can't be solved by us because it's really someone else's problem! That's important to realize. Tell us about the problem without mentioning anyone's name whether it's your problem or a problem that actually belongs to someone else."

Culminate the sharing phase by asking these and/or your own discussion questions to help the students reflect on their learning:

1. *Were some of our problems really other peoples' problems?*
2. *If the problem is really someone else's problem, and you didn't do anything to cause it, do you have any responsibility to solve it?*
3. *Do some problems ever become easier to solve if you "let them be" for a while?*
4. *Did you get any ideas from this session for solving your problem?*

Close the session by thanking the students for their participation and for speaking honestly and listening respectfully.

EXTEND THE LEARNING

Action Plan for Solving Problems – Teach the students these four simple steps for problem solving. Ask them to take notes and ask questions on the steps as you present and discuss each one.

STEP 1. DESCRIBE THE PROBLEM:

Know exactly what the problem is and decide if it is really your problem or someone else's. You can't solve a problem unless you clearly know what the problem is, and if it's not really your problem you can't solve it either. Try not to be confused by the problem. Writing down a description of the problem can help you understand it better.

STEP 2. LIST ALL THE POSSIBLE WAYS TO SOLVE THE PROBLEM:

Even if some solutions seem silly, it's okay. At this point you want to be as creative and open in your thinking as you can. It's also a good idea to write down the ideas you come up with. That way you won't forget any of them before you make up your mind. And remember, asking for help can lead to a solution.

STEP 3. CONSIDER HOW EACH REASONABLE SOLUTION WILL AFFECT YOU AND THE OTHER PEOPLE INVOLVED:

If you don't know how someone else will be affected, it is best to ask. Responsible solutions don't harm you or anyone else.

STEP 4. CHOOSE THE SOLUTION YOU THINK IS BEST AND TRY IT OUT:

If your solution works congratulate yourself. If it doesn't try the next best solution until you find one that works. Remember, problems are normal and everybody has them. It is just part of life. The important thing is to solve your problems as well as you can!

I Had a Problem I Solved In a Positive Way

This last topic relating to problem solving concludes the series on a positive note. By telling about their own positive solutions to problems they have had, the students will likely accept the fact that "we all have problems" and that positive solutions can usually be found.

Begin the session by introducing the topic then elaborate on the topic in your own words by saying something like this:

"Think about some kind of a problem that you had once that you solved in a positive way. Tell us about the problem and how you solved it. Solving problems in a positive way means you and maybe others were helped by the solution and no one got hurt in any way. Also, tell us how you felt when you found your solution was working?"

Culminate the sharing phase by asking these and/or your own discussion questions to help the students reflect on their learning:

1. *What ideas did you get for solving problems in positive ways?*
2. *Can you think of other positive ways to solve some of the problems we described?*

Close the session by thanking the students for their participation and for speaking honestly and listening respectfully.

I Made a Decision That Was Easy to Make

Today the students will enter the topic realm of decision-making, and will begin by telling about a decision they made that caused them little difficulty.

Begin the session by introducing the topic then elaborate on the topic in your own words by saying something like this:

"Think about a time when you had to make some kind of decision that was easy to make. It could have been about almost anything—a purchase, saving money, a project, a gift for someone or a gift for yourself. Whatever it was, tell us about it and how you felt about your choice later on."

Culminate the sharing phase by asking these and/or your own discussion questions to help the students reflect on their learning:

1. *Are all decisions that we make easy?*
2. *What makes some decisions difficult?*

Close the session by thanking the students for their participation and for speaking honestly and listening respectfully.

When I Did Not Get to Share In Making The Decision

This session provides the students with an opportunity to articulate their feelings and the reasons for how they feel when they are not permitted to share in the decision-making process. One of the major benefits of today's activity is that by increasing the students' communicative skills, their ability to constructively negotiate at a verbal level becomes strengthened. As the students' communicative skills increase, they can enter into more meaningful discussions about the decision-making process. They will be much less prone to resort to unhelpful behavior as a way of expressing their feelings when they are not included in decision-making.

Begin the session by introducing the topic then elaborate on the topic in your own words by saying something like this:

"Think of a time when some kind of decision needed to be made that affected you but you were not asked to participate by giving your opinion. Instead other people (it isn't important who) made the decision and you did not get to share in the process. If you feel comfortable tell us about the decision and how you felt about not being included."

Culminate the sharing phase by asking these and/or your own discussion questions to help the students reflect on their learning:

1. *Is it useful to be able to talk about your feelings in situations like this?*

2. *With your growing abilities to explain your opinion and feelings, what could you do the next time you might get left out of making a decision that will affect you?*

3. *Are there times when others, like parents and teachers, should make decisions without your input that will affect you?*

Close the session by thanking the students for their participation and for speaking honestly and listening respectfully.

When I Got to Share In Making The Decision

One of the key ingredients in social relationships is the degree to which people share in making decisions. When people share equally in the decision-making process they feel important and respected.

The purpose of this activity is to bring sharply into each student's awareness an understanding of this wish to share in decision-making and to continue to promote the language necessary to articulately express feelings about this focal issue in social relationships.

Begin the session by introducing the topic then elaborate on the topic in your own words by saying something like this:

"Think about a time when a decision was going to be made that would affect you and you were asked to tell what you thought would work out best. You were consulted, and what you said was taken into consideration. Tell us how it made you feel and what happened."

Culminate the sharing phase by asking these and/or your own discussion questions to help the students reflect on their learning:

1. *If you are in charge of some situation that involves other people and a decision needs to be made that will affect them, what would be a fair thing for you to do?*

2. *What are some of the benefits of shared decision-making? What are some of the difficulties?*

Close the session by thanking the students for their participation and for speaking honestly and listening respectfully.

I Didn't Want to Have to Make a Decision

This topic is a very important one. Similar to not wanting to face problems, people often don't want to be committed to decisions. It is an issue that everyone has to deal with at one time or another. The young person who understands that sometimes he or she must make decisions is far ahead of many people who do not seriously grapple with this reality until later on in life.

(Very often individuals will say that they had no feelings about situations like this which is consistent with the fact that they were probably making themselves as unaware as possible to minimize discomfort. Discuss with the students how people tend to do this sometimes, yet have to face making decisions that are hard to make at one time or another.)

Begin the session by introducing the topic then elaborate on the topic in your own words by saying something like this:

"Think about a time when you felt you were put on the spot in some kind of a situation. Possibly your friends wanted you to do something but you didn't want to do it, so you felt trapped. Or, possibly you were having a hard time choosing between two things. Tell us about how you felt when you didn't want to have to make a decision and how you feel about what happened now."

Culminate the sharing phase by asking these and/or your own discussion questions to help the students reflect on their learning:

1. What usually happens when we just don't make any kind of decision at all?
2. Is it possible to rush too quickly into a decision before waiting to make sure of what's really going on?

Close the session by thanking the students for their participation and for speaking honestly and listening respectfully.

I Stuck By a Difficult Decision I Made

Today's Sharing Circle follows well the former one because it helps clarify the meaning of the first culminating question from that session. Students gain self-reliance when they are enabled to share experiences and their feelings with each other about having the courage to make tough decisions and to stick by them. This session also allows the students to contemplate how circumstances often get worse when decisions are put off.

Begin the session by introducing the topic then elaborate on the topic in your own words by saying something like this:

"Remember the first question we discussed at the end of our last Sharing Circle? It was 'When you keep from making a decision – that's a decision.' Then we talked about what that means. Our topic today asks us to tell each other about how you had the courage to make a tough decision and even more courage to stick by it. This means you had the strength to make a necessary decision and not ignore the matter and put it off. Your decision might have been about finishing something you started, helping someone who needed and wanted your help, things you could do for your health, or another matter that concerns your life. Tell us about the decision and how you feel about yourself as you stick to it."

Culminate the sharing phase by asking these and/or your own discussion questions to help the students reflect on their learning:

1. *What can happen when people pretend that there isn't a problem and keep from making a decision?*
2. *What can happen when they don't stick by important decisions that they make?*

Close the session by thanking the students for their participation and for speaking honestly and listening respectfully.

I Thought It Over and Then Decided

This is a very important Sharing Circle because it reinforces the concept that consideration should precede decisions if they are going to be effective and responsible ones. The students receive dual benefits in this session by first focusing on this value, and second, by telling about a time when they effectively and responsibly thought something over before making a decision.

Begin the session by introducing the topic then elaborate on the topic in your own words by saying something like this:

"Think of a time when you made a decision that you thought over carefully first. Doing this can be very helpful. Not doing it can cause regrets. Tell us about your thoughts and feelings that went into making your decision and how you feel about it now."

Culminate the sharing phase by asking this and/or your own discussion questions to help the students reflect on their learning:

1. *Someone once said, "When you keep from making a decision – that's a decision." What do you think this means?"*
2. *What do you think people who don't want to make a decision are feeling?*

Close the session by thanking the students for their participation and for speaking honestly and listening respectfully.

EXTEND THE LEARNING

Making Good Decisions – Help the students develop an understanding of how to make good decisions by reading through and discussing these decision-making steps. Ask the students to take notes and ask questions as you discuss each step.

STEP 1. DEFINE THE DECISION TO BE MADE:

Write a description of the decision you'll be making. Revisit it, and keep it in mind while you're going through the remaining steps. You may find that your description needs to be changed as you discover new information.

STEP 2. KNOW WHAT IS IMPORTANT TO YOU AND WHAT YOU WANT TO ACCOMPLISH:

This involves such things as your likes and dislikes, your values and interests. Most important it involves having goals. You want to make sure your decisions align with your goals, because you don't want a decision to get you off track from an important goal you want to achieve.

STEP 3. STUDY THE INFORMATION YOU ALREADY HAVE. GET AND STUDY NEW INFORMATION TOO:

You can get information by talking to people, visiting places, watching TV, researching on the internet, and reading. Once you have the information, you must be able to evaluate it. If two people tell you to do opposite things, how are you going to know which is right? What if neither is right? What if both are right?

STEP 4. LOOK AT EACH ALTERNATIVE AND ASK YOURSELF WHAT WILL HAPPEN TO YOU AND OTHER PEOPLE INVOLVED IF YOU CHOOSE IT:

A good way to consider the advantages and disadvantages of each alternative is by looking into the future. Ask yourself what will probably happen if you choose each alternative.

STEP 5. MAKE A DECISION

STEP 6. DEVELOP A PLAN FOR PUTTING YOUR DECISION INTO ACTION:

Not every decision requires an action plan, but big ones usually do. Something like deciding to go to college requires decisions and planning to make sure it happens.

I Observed a Conflict

The students will begin their discussions about conflict management and resolution with this topic. In this session they will tell about conflicts that they witnessed. By discussing conflicts that they were not involved in, the students will be given an opportunity in this initial session to improve their understanding of the dynamics in conflicts and their outcomes with some degree of objectivity. In the next sessions they will talk about conflict situations that they experienced personally.

Begin the session by introducing the topic then elaborate on the topic in your own words by saying something like this:

"Think about a time when you saw two people (or more) get into a conflict. Be very sure not to tell us who was involved in the conflict. Just tell us how it got started and what happened. You might add how being an observer made you feel then and now. It would be interesting also to hear whether or not the conflict you observed was settled well or not so well."

Culminate the sharing phase by asking these and/or your own discussion questions to help the students reflect on their learning:

1. *Did you hear about any actions that could be helpful for managing and resolving conflicts well? If so, what were they?*
2. *What were some actions that did not help settle these conflicts in healthy ways?*

Close the session by thanking the students for their participation and for speaking honestly and listening respectfully.

EXTEND THE LEARNING

As the students are beginning a series of Sharing Circle topics dealing with conflict, help them understand that conflicts are a normal part of life. Some conflicts are terrible and lead to hurt feelings and even hurt bodies. Other conflicts aren't so bad. Some can even lead to good things. But in order for something productive to come out of conflict it has to be managed well. Here are some pro-social conflict management strategies that help the students develop an understanding of specific actions they can take to help manage a conflict positively.

LISTEN

Often people get into conflicts because they don't really listen to each other or they misunderstand what they hear. So really try to listen to the other person's point of view. Tune in to words, and feelings too. Pay attention, don't interrupt, and let the other person know that you are listening.

TRY TO COMPROMISE

If you offer to give up some of what you want first, and the other person agrees to as well, then you can both have at least part of what you want. That's a compromise.

TAKE TURNS

Some conflicts happen because two people want the same thing at the same time. Show the other person that you are willing to be second sometimes. Flip a coin, draw straws, guess a number between one and ten, or simply say "you go first".

PUT IT OFF

If you are mad, tired, hungry, or in a hurry– or you think the other person is – wait! Put off dealing with the conflict until later. You can say something like: *"I want to settle this, but now is not the time. Let's wait until after lunch. Everything seems to be going wrong. I'm too tired to think straight. Could we get back to this later?"*

(Continued)

GET HELP

Bring someone into the conflict who can help settle it. This may sound like tattling, but it's not. Tattling is trying to get the other person in trouble. Getting help is asking another person to help straighten out the conflict. Often a person not involved in the conflict can see things the people in conflict can't and can come up with positive solutions that will work for everyone.

PROBLEM SOLVE

Calmly and without any blaming, discuss the problem and try to find a resolution that is acceptable to both you and the other person. This could be a good time to bring in a neutral person as a mediator to help you find a solution.

EXPRESS REGRET

Let the other person know that you are sorry the conflict happened. You don't have to admit you are wrong or that the conflict is your fault. Lot's of times it just really helps when you say things like: "It's too bad this happened." "I know you're upset and I feel bad about it."

I Got Blamed for Something That I Didn't Do

Impulsive handling of frustration can lead to more frustration. The person who blames another is usually frustrated and angry. These kinds of feelings can lead to unreasonable behavior like unfair blaming of others, which in turn, causes those who are blamed to feel frustrated and reactive. Today the students will discuss the frustration that accompanies receiving blame when they are not guilty. By discussing this topic they will be focusing on their own feelings when they are unfairly treated and how this does at one time or another seem to happen to everyone.

Begin the session by introducing the topic then elaborate on the topic in your own words by saying something like this:

"Has anyone ever put the blame on you for something that you didn't do? Without telling who did it, tell us about what happened and how you felt. Also think about the emotions of the person who did the blaming and tell us what you think those emotions might have been?"

Culminate the sharing phase by asking these and/or your own discussion questions to help the students reflect on their learning:

1. *What are some of the constructive ways to handle a situation like this that you heard in this session, or that you can think of?*
2. *If you feel like blaming someone for something they did that upset you, what should you do first?*

Close the session by thanking the students for their participation and for speaking honestly and listening respectfully.

I Got Involved In a Conflict Because Something Unfair Was Happening to Someone Else

Today the students will again discuss their involvement in a conflict because of unfair treatment, but in this case they are not the victim, someone else is. This is a complex issue. By discussing it, the students will have an opportunity to realize that sometimes conflicts are unavoidable and our involvement in them is the responsible thing to do and sometimes it isn't. They will examine complexities in these situations: when becoming involved with someone else's problem is "none of our business" and what are the most constructive ways to intervene when we decide to.

Begin the session by introducing the topic then elaborate on the topic in your own words by saying something like this:

"Think of a time when you saw something happening when one person or a group was being hurt in some way by another person or group and you didn't think it was right so you got involved. Without telling us who the people were, tell us how you were feeling and about what happened before and after you got involved. You might add whether you think you did the right thing and, if not, how you would act if a similar situation occurred."

Note: Do not evaluate the students' responses. Rather, in a general way, discuss how sometimes it is hard to tell whether or not our interventions are really helpful or just unnecessary interference. Sometimes people do need help of this kind from someone else and to give it very often takes a lot of courage. Discuss also how there are various ways to intervene and each situation requires a careful analysis if the intervention is to be effective.

Culminate the sharing phase by asking these and/or your own discussion questions to help the students reflect on their learning:

1. *When do you think it is right and necessary to intervene when someone is being treated unfairly, and when isn't it?*
2. *If you get involved in a situation like this, is there just one way to do it?*
3. *What are some ways that will not hurt anyone unnecessarily?*

Close the session by thanking the students for their participation and for speaking honestly and listening respectfully.

I Got Into a Fight Because I Was Already Feeling Bad

Today's session has the students consider how the way we feel can cause us to behave in certain ways. When we feel good the behaviors that usually result are friendly, cooperative, and helpful. But when we feel bad we very often manifest negative behaviors unless we become aware of our feelings and our urges and stop ourselves from committing acts that will hurt or disturb someone else.

Begin the session by introducing the topic then elaborate on the topic in your own words by saying something like this:

"Think of a time when you got into a conflict and, as you look back on it, you realize that it probably happened because you were already feeling bad. Your feelings may have made you act in certain ways that led to the conflict. Tell us how it happened, how you felt and how you feel about it now."

Culminate the sharing phase by asking these and/or your own discussion questions to help the students reflect on their learning:

1. *Do the chances of a conflict increase when the number of people who are feeling bad increases?*
2. *Do you have to act the way you feel?*
3. *How important is it to think about how you feel before you respond with hurtful behaviors?*

Close the session by thanking the students for their participation and for speaking honestly and listening respectfully.

I Felt Like Saying Something, But I Didn't

Today the students will talk about times when they behaved pro-socially. Sometimes we feel like speaking our truth and we stop ourselves but it may have been better to speak. Many other times, however, we can be fairly sure that if we impulsively say something we're thinking the result will be hurt feelings or anger. By speaking our feelings and thoughts responsibly, without overtly or covertly attacking we can avoid non-productive conflicts. Today's Sharing Circle addresses this second kind of conscious verbal restraint.

Begin the session by introducing the topic then elaborate on the topic in your own words by saying something like this:

"Have you ever been in some situation where you felt like saying something to someone but you stopped yourself – not because you were afraid but because you realized at the time that to say it would only cause hurt or anger? By not saying it, you may have kept an unnecessary conflict from occurring. Without telling us who was involved, tell us about what was happening and what you felt like saying and why you stopped yourself. Also tell us how you feel about it now."

Culminate the sharing phase by asking these and/or your own discussion questions to help the students reflect on their learning:

1. *Do you always have to say what you're thinking?*
2. *When do you think it is best to go ahead and state your thoughts and feelings?*
3. *How do we seem to feel now about how we controlled ourselves from hurting others or making them angry with our words?*

Close the session by thanking the students for their participation and for speaking honestly and listening respectfully.

A Time When Somebody Put Me Down and I Handled It Well

This session is a complex and challenging one. Today the students will discuss how they consciously chose to handle a difficult situation responsibly and not because they were afraid. Since each person is responsible only for what he or she says, we are all vulnerable to verbal violence that comes from others who we can't control. In the session just prior to this one, the students discussed how they used their self-control to keep from saying something that probably would have brought about a negative outcome. But sometimes other people say things to us that make us feel hurt or angry. In these situations it is even harder to keep one's perspective and self control. When we are able to keep from counter-attacking we are demonstrating, in perhaps the most difficult of contexts, our human capacity to behave rationally – to be in charge of our own behavior, despite the way we feel like behaving.

Begin the session by introducing the topic then elaborate on the topic in your own words by saying something like this:

"Have you ever had someone put you down and you felt like hurting them back in a physical or verbal way, but you didn't – not because you were scared to, but because you knew that an unnecessary conflict would probably result and you didn't want that to happen? Without telling us who put you down, tell us how it happened, how you felt, and how you handled it."

Culminate the sharing phase by asking this and/or your own discussion questions to help the students reflect on their learning:

1. *How do you feel about what you did now?*
2. *What would you call the ability to handle it well when somebody puts you down?*

Close the session by thanking the students for their participation and for speaking honestly and listening respectfully.

I Was Angry At One Person, But I Took It Out On Someone Else

Today the students will discuss the defense mechanism, displacement – a behavior that frequently leads to conflicts. By discussing this topic the students will have an opportunity to understand how displacement works and thereby recognize it in themselves and in other people when it occurs. This kind of recognition can lead to certain benefits. Sometimes a student will take out his or her frustrations on a weaker or less influential individual or object (such as a little brother or the cat) instead of the real source of their frustrations. Discussing this topic and gaining the awareness that it may bring may equip the students to purposefully change their behavior when the urge to displace resentment is felt. A further benefit may be gained when they realize what someone else is actually doing when he or she is displacing anger upon them. Awareness gained about displacement may aid in realizing that there is nothing inherently bad or wrong with them when they are unfairly made the victim.

Begin the session by introducing the topic then elaborate on the topic in your own words by saying something like this:

"Have you ever been angry at one person or group of people and you would have liked to take out your anger on them, but for some reason you didn't? Instead, you took it out on someone, or something, else—like your little sister or the cat? Tell us about what happened that got you upset and how you took out the upset on the wrong target. It may take some courage to tell us how you were feeling at the time but it is important information. It would also be informative to hear how you feel about what happened now."

Note: As the students respond to the topic, let them know that you appreciate their courage to tell about something of this nature. In a matter-of-fact way, reflect to them that displacement is a very universal phenomenon; probably everybody has experienced it as the unaware perpetrator or as the victim. Some of the students may prefer to just listen today, due to the challenging nature of the topic.

Culminate the sharing phase by asking these and/or your own discussion questions to help the students reflect on their learning:

1. *Do you think that it is fair for people to take their anger out on someone who didn't cause it in the first place?*

2. *Why do you think people sometimes stop themselves from taking out their anger on the one who caused it and take it out on someone else?*

3. *When people attack the wrong target do you think they realize why they are doing it?*

Close the session by thanking the students for their participation and for speaking honestly and listening respectfully.

A Good Idea I Got From Someone In the Group for Handling a Conflict

This is a very open-ended Sharing Circle inviting the students to tell each other what they learned from one another about constructive and responsible handling of potential and actual conflicts. By doing this, the students will again receive positive reinforcement for their positive actions, this time directly from their peers.

Begin the session by introducing the topic. Next, focus on a student and tell him or her about something he or she said in one of the sessions on conflict management and resolution that you considered to be a good idea. Then ask:

"Did anyone else hear a good idea from another member of our group about how to help keep an unnecessary conflict from occurring or how to handle a conflict that was already happening? If so, tell the person and the rest of us what it was."

Note: If any students are not named and told about a good idea they shared, be sure to tell each one something yourself that you appreciated so that each student will be acknowledged.

Culminate the sharing phase by asking these and/or your own discussion questions to help the students reflect on their learning:

1. *How did it feel to acknowledge someone for a good idea and how did it feel to be acknowledged?*
2. *Can every conflict be avoided, or should it be?*

Close the session by thanking the students for their participation and for speaking honestly and listening respectfully.

Something I've Done (or Could Do) to Improve Our World

This last topic asks the students to focus on their personal contribution to the betterment of their community and world. Through discussions of this sort students can begin to see a connection between their own actions and their effects on the society and world they live in.

Begin the session by introducing the topic then elaborate on the topic in your own words by saying something like this:

"Can you think of a time when you did something that you felt really helped, even in a small way, to improve the world we live in? Perhaps you helped improve a condition of some kind on your street or in your community. Maybe you helped change something you thought was wrong. Or perhaps you did something to help the environment, like taking care not to waste valuable resources like water or electricity. Maybe you are careful to treat all animals with care. If you can't think of something you've already done, perhaps you can think of something you would like to do in the future, either independently or with a group."

Culminate the sharing phase by asking these and/or your own discussion questions to help the students reflect on their learning:

1. *How can we create an atmosphere in this community (or in this country) that will encourage people to take action to improve things?*

2. *How do you feel when you do something that helps improve our world?*

3. *How do your values help determine what you view as important and contributing to a better world?*

Close the session by thanking the students for their participation and for speaking honestly and listening respectfully.

www.ingramcontent.com/pod-product-compliance
Lightning Source LLC
Chambersburg PA
CBHW081218230426
43666CB00015B/2781